www.ACIprep.com

Master SAT Vocabulary

in 10 Weeks

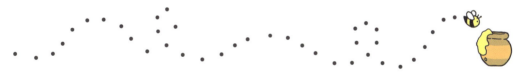

ACI SINCE 1987 INSTITUTE

All inquiries should be addressed to:
ACI Institute
1041 S. Garfield Ave. #101
Alhambra, CA 91801
www.ACIprep.com

ISBN-13: 978-0-615-29351-6
ISBN-10: 0-615-29351-4

Art Designer: Jessica Sheu
Production Coordinator: May Shih

Manufactured in the United States of America

TABLE OF CONTENTS

Regular Level

Answer Keys

TABLE OF CONTENTS

Advanced Level

Answer Keys

Introduction

Who We Are

ACI Institute, since its establishment in 1987, has excelled in providing quality prepatory courses and individualized counseling for students seeking to be accepted into their dream schools. As one of the leading institutes of its kind in Southern California, ACI has committed itself to helping students gain access to all the tools they need to fulfill their academic goals. With help from qualified staff, educators and counselors, many students have been accepted to some of the top schools in the country, including Harvard, Yale, Stanford, MIT, Cal Tech, UC Berkeley and UCLA.

What is the secret to its success? ACI motivates students, often through its rigorous but effective curriculum in order to help students achieve high marks on standardized tests such as the CST, PSAT, SAT I, SAT II, GRE, and various APs. After-school classes and individual tutoring opportunities further strengthen a student's skills in Math, English, History and Science. As a result, ACI students feel more confident and score much higher on their grades overall.

In addition to a strong emphasis on academics, ACI is dedicated to helping not only the student but the family as well to understand and anticipate those problem areas that arise along the complicated road to college. In doing so, ACI seeks to do its part in preparing the next generation to venture into a world filled with opportunities for success.

About this Book

Without a doubt, one sign of intellectual growth is an ever growing vocabulary. Studies show that colleges, companies and corporations value those who are able to communicate clearly and effectively. To do so, you must have the extensive vocabulary needed to convey your ideas accurately to others. By using the words you learn in this book, you will impress others with your ability to communicate. In short, intellectual maturity is directly proportional to your word power.

For many of you, this book becomes your first step in improving your word power. Through years of examining SAT tests and understanding students' needs, we have sifted through thousands of vocabulary words found in the SAT and compiled 1,500 essential words for success. That amount may seem like quite a bit, but by following the plan found in this book and with the help of your ACI instructor and counselor, you will build your word skills significantly over the next few months. In no time, you will have at your disposal a good foundation to communicate successfully in any career.

It is our hope that students will not be daunted by the SAT, but rather, will use this book to expand their vocabulary and master the test. Most students struggle with the verbal section, not because they don't understand the logic behind the questions, but because they are not familiar with the words. After going through this book, you'll be one step closer to that high score you want to achieve. Good luck in your quest to expand your mind and vocabulary!

About the SAT

The SAT has gone through numerous changes over the years. Currently, the SAT is based on three different sections of 800 points each, for a perfect score of 2400. The three different sections test verbal, grammar and math skills. Despite all the various changes, one thing has remained constant: the demand to know vocabulary words. Unfortunately, there is no other surefire way to increase your verbal scores without expanding your vocabulary bank. The good news is that vocabulary is not as infinite as students may think. We have combined all the most important words in this handy book.

According to the College Board,[1] the official administrators of the SAT, this standardized college entrance test helps colleges and universities identify students who are able to succeed at their institutions and to connect students with educational opportunities beyond high school. However, it is important for students to understand that the SAT is just one factor among many that colleges use to evaluate their applicants. Keep the test in perspective and understand that it is only part of a comprehensive admission process that also recognizes other factors, such as extracurricular activities and high school grades. Nonetheless, educators trust the SAT as a useful part of the college application process since the SAT Is the most researched standardized admissions exam, the standard in reliability and validity, and an internationally recognized, accurate measure of college readiness and scholarship potential.

---

[1] "College Board." SAT I Reasoning Test. <www.collegeboard.com>.

How to Use this Book:

Dear student,

You have just begun the ambitious task of mastering over 1000 SAT vocabulary words in only ten weeks. Along with patience and diligence, the format of this book will help make that task manageable.

This comprehensive program includes a total of 1500 words. The regular level consists of ten essential lessons to familiarize you with the most fundamental SAT words. Each lesson consists of 100 words per week, or 20 words every weekday. For faster progress, you can challenge yourself with the advanced level by studying an additional fifty words per week.

At the end of each weekly lesson, a crossword puzzle and a short quiz consisting of words from the preceding chapter may be found. These puzzles and quizzes are intended for review, after the words and their definitions have been studied and committed to memory. Answers to these puzzles and quizzes are in the back of the book.

Of course, continue to keep this book on your shelf to refresh your memory with frequent review. Good luck!

- The ACI Team

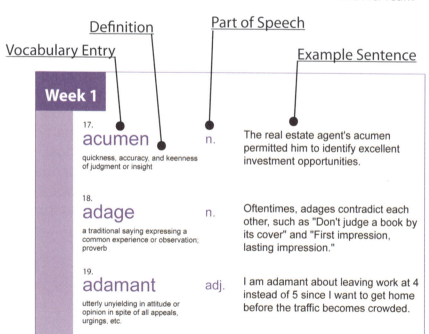

Definition   Part of Speech

Vocabulary Entry   Example Sentence

Week 1

17.
acumen   n.
quickness, accuracy, and keenness of judgment or insight

The real estate agent's acumen permitted him to identify excellent investment opportunities.

18.
adage   n.
a traditional saying expressing a common experience or observation; proverb

Oftentimes, adages contradict each other, such as "Don't judge a book by its cover" and "First impression, lasting impression."

19.
adamant   adj.
utterly unyielding in attitude or opinion in spite of all appeals, urgings, etc.

I am adamant about leaving work at 4 instead of 5 since I want to get home before the traffic becomes crowded.

Crossword Puzzle

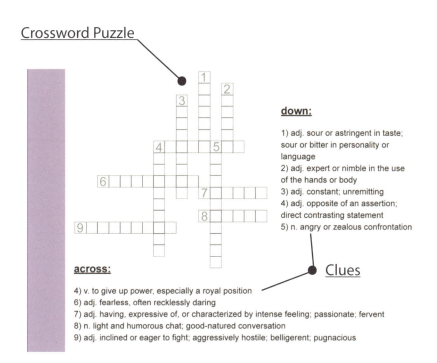

down:

1) adj. sour or astringent in taste; sour or bitter in personality or language
2) adj. expert or nimble in the use of the hands or body
3) adj. constant; unremitting
4) adj. opposite of an assertion; direct contrasting statement
5) n. angry or zealous confrontation

Clues

across:

4) v. to give up power, especially a royal position
6) adj. fearless, often recklessly daring
7) adj. having, expressive of, or characterized by intense feeling; passionate; fervent
8) n. light and humorous chat; good-natured conversation
9) adj. inclined or eager to fight; aggressively hostile; belligerent; pugnacious

Self-Quiz

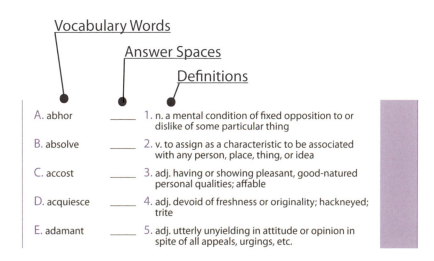

Vocabulary Words

Answer Spaces

Definitions

A. abhor _____ 1. n. a mental condition of fixed opposition to or dislike of some particular thing

B. absolve _____ 2. v. to assign as a characteristic to be associated with any person, place, thing, or idea

C. accost _____ 3. adj. having or showing pleasant, good-natured personal qualities; affable

D. acquiesce _____ 4. adj. devoid of freshness or originality; hackneyed; trite

E. adamant _____ 5. adj. utterly unyielding in attitude or opinion in spite of all appeals, urgings, etc.

300pts

100pts

Week 1

abet

banal

"Knowledge is power,
but enthusiasm pulls the switch."
- Ivern Ball

verb

adj.

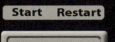

1.
abdicate   v.
to give up power, especially a royal position

When the king abdicated his throne, the people reacted mournfully, for he had led their country wisely.

2.
abet   v.
to aid, promote, or encourage the commission of (an offense)

Jeff blames his cousin for abetting him in betting on the wrong horse and losing a lot of money!

3.
abhor   v.
to regard with extreme disgust; detest utterly, loathe

The young child abhorred the horrible taste of brussel sprouts.

4.
abrade   v.
to wear off or down by scraping or rubbing

Sandpaper works well because individual grains abrade the raw edge of wood or any other soft surface.

5.
abridge   v.
to shorten by omissions while retaining the basic contents

The engineer submitted an abridged version of the plan for building a bridge.

6.
absolve   v.
to free from guilt or blame or their consequences

The priest absolved her sins but still could not help solve her problems.

7.
abstruse   adj.
hard to understand

Professor Griffith's last class was so abstruse that all the students demanded that he repeat what he said more clearly.

8.
abyss   n.
a deep, immeasurable space, gulf, or cavity; vast chasm

The deepest regions of the ocean remain an unexplored abyss.

9.

accede
v.

to give consent, approval, or adherence; agree; assent

The two lawyers acceded to the court's demand that they turn over all evidence to the prosecuting attorneys for review.

10.

accommodate
v.

to do a kindness or a favor to; oblige

Most hotels try to accommodate their regular customers, giving them the finest rooms available.

11.

accord
n.

an agreement; harmony

Her actions were not in accord with her beliefs.

12.

accost
v.

to approach and speak to aggressively

Dinah accosted the salesgirl, demanding that the store carry a larger size.

13.

acerbic
adj.

sour or astringent in taste; sour or bitter in personality or language

Grouchy old Bertha was no fun to meet when she would use such acerbic words just to ask for a glass of water.

14.

acquiesce
v.

to comply; submit

After deliberating for a few hours, Jason finally acquiesced to his sister's demands to keep her quiet.

15.

acquisitive
adj.

eager to acquire and retain ideas or information

Tyler has an acquisitive mind, taking everything he has done as a learning opportunity.

16.

acrimonious
adj.

caustic, stinging, or bitter in nature, speech, behavior, etc.

In Romeo and Juliet, the Capulets and Montagues can never trust each other, speaking about each other in acrimonious words.

WEEK 1
WEEK 2
WEEK 3
WEEK 4
WEEK 5
WEEK 6
WEEK 7
WEEK 8
WEEK 9
WEEK 10

REGULAR

17.

acumen n.

quickness, accuracy, and keenness of judgment or insight

The real estate agent's acumen permitted him to identify excellent investment opportunities.

18.

adage n.

a traditional saying expressing a common experience or observation; proverb

Oftentimes, adages contradict each other, such as "Don't judge a book by its cover" and "First impression, lasting impression."

19.

adamant adj.

utterly unyielding in attitude or opinion in spite of all appeals, urgings, etc.

You may think I'm stubborn, but I say I'm only adamant about getting straight A's.

20.

adept adj.

very skilled; proficient; expert

Gymnasts are often adept at performing extremely difficult and demanding maneuvers on the balance beam.

21.

adhere v.

to stick together; to remain devoted to; to be in accordance with something such as rules

The contract demanded that new workers strictly adhere to the new office dress code.

22.

adjunct n.

something added to another thing but not essential to it; (adj.) joined or associated, esp. in a subordinate relationship

Medication can be a useful adjunct to physical therapy and a regular exercise regimen.

23.

admonish v.

to caution, advise, or counsel against something

Dad admonished Terry about his leaving the house without informing either him or his mother when he would return.

24.

adroit adj.

expert or nimble in the use of the hands or body

Surgeons have to be adroit when performing intricate surgery on repairing muscle tissue.

25.

advent n.

a coming into place, view, or being; arrival

The election of 2008 was the advent, to many, of a new era in race relations in the US with the election of Barack Obama.

26.

advocate n.

a person who speaks or writes in support or defense of a person, cause, etc.; (v.) to speak or write in favor of; support or urge by argument; recommend publicly

Al Gore was a strong advocate for a sound, green environmental program.

27.

aesthetic adj.

pertaining to beauty, taste, or the fine arts

The beautiful paintings Stacey did for the art show reveal her aesthetic sensibility.

28.

affable adj.

pleasantly easy to approach and to talk to; friendly; cordial; warmly polite

Despite her husband's rude and distant personality, Francine was affable, welcoming guests in with open arms.

29.

affiliate v.

to bring into close association or connection

My mother warned me not to affiliate myself with the strange family that had moved in next door.

30.

affluence n.

abundance of money, property, and other material goods; riches; wealth

People who live in Beverly Hills and San Marino are noted for their affluence.

31.

aggravate v.

to make worse or more severe; intensify, as anything evil, disorderly, or troublesome

When Leon began jogging that next morning, he aggravated his ankle injury sustained from yesterday's tennis game.

32.

aggregate adj.

formed by the conjunction or collection of particulars into a whole mass or sum; total; combined

Even though Elisa had support from her coach, she received no help from the aggregate members of the debate squad for losing the competition.

WEEK 1
WEEK 2
WEEK 3
WEEK 4
WEEK 5
WEEK 6
WEEK 7
WEEK 8
WEEK 9
WEEK 10

REGULAR

33.

agile

adj.

quick and well-coordinated in movement

Most monkeys are agile creatures, freely swinging from tree to tree in the jungle.

34.

allege

v.

to assert to be true, especially in a formal manner, as in court

The victim alleged that the burglar broke into her home while she was sleeping soundly in her room.

35.

alleviate

v.

to make easier to endure; lessen in severity

Most over-the-counter drugs simply alleviate symptoms of a cold rather than cure it altogether.

36.

allot

v.

to divide or distribute by share or portion; distribute or parcel out

The city alloted a lot of money for fixing the streets.

37.

allude

v.

to refer to incidentally, or by suggestion

Mary could not help alluding to the suspicious note she found in William's coat pocket.

38.

aloof

adv.

at a distance, esp. in feeling or interest; apart; (adj.) reserved; indifferent

She remained aloof, standing by herself at the party, keeping an eye on everyone who might approach her so that she could move into another room.

39.

altercation

n.

angry or zealous confrontation

The divorced couple often engaged in altercations in the middle of the night, disturbing their neighbors' slumber.

40.

altruism

n.

the principle or practice of unselfish concern for or devotion to the welfare of others

Maxine was given a lifetime award for her spirit of altruism in forming the Children's Hospital and advocating for fair treatment of poor families in the community.

41.

ambidextrous adj.

able to use both hands equally well

Cecilia was amazed at how ambidextrous Juan was: he writes with his right hand and paints with his left.

42.

ambiguous adj.

open to or having several possible meanings or interpretations

No one could read Darice's handwriting, and those who could, did not understand her ambiguous instructions directing them to the ice cream parlor.

43.

ambivalence n.

uncertainty or fluctuation, esp. when caused by inability to make a choice or by a simultaneous desire to say or do two opposite or conflicting things

Martin was known for his ambivalence; he couldn't even decide which shoe to put on first.

44.

amble v.

to go at a slow, easy pace; stroll

Most young couples love to spend a quiet afternoon ambling in the park, enjoying the warm air and romantic scenery.

45.

amenable adj.

ready or willing to answer, act, agree, or yield; open to influence, persuasion, or advice; agreeable; submissive

I am amenable to the idea that we should work together on selling the company's new product.

46.

amiable adj.

having or showing pleasant, good-natured personal qualities

Don't you appreciate amiable people who make lousy days better with just a simple smile?

47.

amicable adj.

characterized by or showing goodwill; friendly; peaceable

The couple came to an amicable agreement over who would spend time with their newly adopted little boy.

48.

amorous adj.

strongly attracted or disposed to showing physical affection; indicating love or sexual expression

At nightfall, the couple was locked in an amorous embrace in the moonlight by the water fountain in the park.

WEEK 1
WEEK 2
WEEK 3
WEEK 4
WEEK 5
WEEK 6
WEEK 7
WEEK 8
WEEK 9
WEEK 10

REGULAR

49.
anarchy n.
a state of society without government or law

Anarchy broke out after the General overthrew the monarchy without setting up a new government.

50.
annex n.
a building added to a larger one; (v.) to add or affix at the end; to add territory

The annex was constructed to provide more classroom space for our growing student body.

51.
annihilate v.
to reduce to utter ruin or nonexistence; destroy utterly

He gleefully laughed at home when, in the game, he annihilated all the enemy invaders and saved the planet.

52.
annotation n.
note created to explain or cite

If you are going to write a research paper, you will have to include annotations.

53.
antecedent n.
a preceding circumstance, event, object, style, phenomenon, etc.; (adj.) preceding; prior

The Model T was the antecedent of many newer makes of cars throughout the 20th century.

54.
antidote n.
a medicine or other remedy for counteracting the effects of poison, disease, etc.; v. to counteract with an antidote

Quinine is an effective antidote to malaria and has helped made the disease rare.

55.
antipathy n.
expression of antagonism or deep dislike

He has such antipathy for New Englanders that he refuses to visit any of the Northeastern states.

56.
antiquated adj.
continued from, resembling, or adhering to the past; old-fashioned

The typewriter in the antique shop was very antiquated.

57.
antithesis
adj.

opposite of an assertion; direct
contrasting statement

Her behavior was the very antithesis
of cowardly.

WEEK
1

WEEK
2

58.
apathy
n.

absence or suppression of passion,
emotion, or excitement

Voter apathy has often been blamed
on an overexposure of the media to
each candidate's faults.

WEEK
3

WEEK
4

59.
appall
v.

to fill or overcome with horror or fear;
dismay

I was appalled when I saw the news of
the poor young child's murder.

WEEK
5

WEEK
6

60.
appease
v.

to soothe by quieting anger or
indignation

Jane hoped to appease her angry
father by offering to help pay for the
damage she had caused to his car.

WEEK
7

WEEK
8

61.
appraise
v.

to estimate the monetary value of;
determine the worth of; assess

Tax officials stopped by earlier today
to appraise the value of the house.

WEEK
9

62.
apprehensive
adj.

uneasy or fearful about something
that might happen

Ophelia was apprehensive about
walking into the old abandoned house.

WEEK
10

63.
arable
adj.

farmable; capable of producing crops

The Midwest has plenty of arable
land; most of the nation's corn is
grown there.

64.
arbitrate
v.

to make a judgment or help to
resolve differences, esp. as a
mediator between two groups or
persons

Mr. Parker, the eminent judge, was
called to arbitrate the talks between
management and labor.

REGULAR

65.
archaic
adj.

marked by the characteristics of an earlier period

"Thee" and "thou" are archaic ways of saying "you."

66.
ardent
adj.

having, expressive of, or characterized by intense feeling; passionate; fervent

True to her conservative form, Mary was an ardent supporter of the Republican candidate for President.

67.
argumentative
adj.

fond of or given to argument and dispute

Benedict was just being argumentative when he said he did not want to mow the lawn because he wanted to watch the Lakers game.

68.
arraign
v.

to call or bring before a court to answer to an indictment

A suspect must be arraigned in court before a trial can begin.

69.
array
v.

to place in proper or desired order

Candy's Candies had a fine array of chocolates just waiting for the hungry customer.

70.
assiduous
adj.

constant; unremitting; hard-working

She worked assiduously, allowing nothing to stand in the way of completing the fifty calculus problems by morning.

71.
assimilate
v.

to take in and incorporate as one's own; absorb

Immigrants slowly assimilated into the culture of New York City in the late 19th and early 20th centuries and began to live similar lives as their American neighbors.

72.
assuage
v.

to make (something burdensome or painful) less intense or severe; to calm

The widow assuaged her grief by devoting all of her time and energy to the upbringing of her beloved children.

73.

astute adj.

of keen penetration or discernment; insightful

I am amazed at how astute that young man is; he can do advanced algebra problems even though he's only 10 years old.

74.

atone v.

to make amends, as for an offense, a crime, or a sin

The worshipers came with their offerings, seeking to atone for the sins of their community.

75.

atrocity n.

a cruel act that causes pain and suffering; behavior that is wicked and inhumane

The Nuremberg trials sought justice for the atrocities committed during the Holocaust.

76.

atrophy n.

wasting away from lack of use, as in a part of the body or the mind

If you don't study, your mind will atrophy.

77.

attribute v.

to assign as a characteristic to be associated with any person, place, thing, or idea

The scholars attributed the newly discovered book of poetry to Shakespeare.

78.

audacious adj.

fearless, often recklessly daring

In an audacious move, the cliff diver somersaulted twice before entering the water.

79.

augment v.

to make larger; enlarge in size, number, strength, or extent; increase

Most coffee drinkers add cream and sugar to augment the flavor of the coffee drinking experience.

80.

auspicious adj.

promising success; highly favorable

Most inaugurations are to be treated as auspicious events, filled with pomp and grandeur.

WEEK 1
WEEK 2
WEEK 3
WEEK 4
WEEK 5
WEEK 6
WEEK 7
WEEK 8
WEEK 9
WEEK 10

81.
austere adj.

severe in manner or appearance;
uncompromising; strict; forbidding

The School Board approved an
austere budget limiting the purchases
of office supplies for the classroom.

82.
autonomous adj.

self-governing; independent; subject
to its own laws only

Because of its segregation from
politics, the Supreme Court is an
autonomous judiciary.

83.
aversion n.

a mental condition of fixed opposition
to or dislike of some particular thing

Alice has an aversion to all foods
made from apples.

84.
avow v.

to declare frankly or openly; own;
acknowledge; confess; admit

He avowed that he would not leave
the campus without gaining
permission from the resident director.

85.
baleful adj.

full of menacing or threatening
influences

The baleful consequences of his
arrest impacted his whole family.

86.
banal adj.

devoid of freshness or originality

No one cared for the banal class in
which the teacher lectured for two
hours straight.

87.
baneful adj.

destructive

Invasion of grasshoppers was baneful
to the crops of the farming community.

88.
banter n.

light and humorous chat;
good-natured conversation

The banter that characters engage in
on situation comedies doesn't seem
very realistic.

89.

barbarous

adj.

uncivilized; wild; savage; crude

The world was shocked at the barbarous acts of the Nazis during the Holocaust.

90.

barrage

n.

overwhelming quantity or explosion of words, blows or criticisms

The mayor was faced with a barrage of criticism when he declared the entire city a no parking zone.

91.

bashful

adj.

uncomfortably shy and easily embarrassed; timid

Penny was bashful when Rick came over to ask her to dance.

92.

bask

v.

to lie in or be exposed to a pleasant warmth

The movie star basked in the attention she received at the movie's premiere.

93.

begrudge

v.

to envy or resent the pleasure or good fortune of (someone)

I'm not begrudging your wanting to retire, but don't you think doing so at 50 might be too young?

94.

beguile

v.

to influence by trickery, flattery, etc.; mislead; delude

Eric was beguiled by her charms into believing that she would always be by his side.

95.

belie

v.

to show to be false; contradict

His shaky hands belied what appeared to be an otherwise calm, cool exterior, suggesting that he might actually fear the confrontation.

96.

bellicose

adj.

inclined or eager to fight; aggressively hostile; belligerent

We should be cautious of world leaders with bellicose attitudes.

WEEK 1
WEEK 2
WEEK 3
WEEK 4
WEEK 5
WEEK 6
WEEK 7
WEEK 8
WEEK 9
WEEK 10

REGULAR

97.

belligerent   adj.

of warlike character; aggressively hostile; bellicose

Don't be so belligerent; I will work with you better if you don't try to fight me.

98.

bemoan   v.

to express distress or grief over

The families bemoaned the long and cold winter that seemed to trap them in their apartment for months.

99.

benediction   n.

a solemn blessing; an expression of good wishes

The priest offered a benediction to the young couple who were having marital problems.

100.

benefactor   n.

a person who confers a benefit; kindly helper

Oscar was well known as a generous benefactor to graduating college students.

A. Fill in the appropriate words using the clues below.

down:

1) adj. sour in taste; sour or bitter in personality or language
2) adj. expert or nimble in the use of the hands or body
3) adj. constant; unremitting; hard working
4) adj. opposite of an assertion; direct contrasting statement
5) n. angry or zealous confrontation

across:

4) v. to give up power, especially a royal position
6) adj. fearless, often recklessly daring
7) adj. having, expressive of, or characterized by intense feeling; passionate; fervent
8) n. light and humorous chat; good-natured conversation
9) adj. inclined or eager to fight; aggressively hostile; belligerent

B. Match the words on the left with their appropriate definitions on the right.

A. abhor _____

1. n. a mental condition of fixed opposition to or dislike of some particular thing

B. absolve _____

2. v. to assign as a characteristic to be associated with any person, place, thing, or idea

C. accost _____

3. adj. having or showing pleasant, good-natured personal qualities

D. acquiesce _____

4. adj. devoid of freshness or originality

E. adamant _____

5. adj. utterly unyielding in attitude or opinion in spite of all appeals, urgings, etc.

F. advent _____

6. v. to make larger; enlarge in size, number, strength, or extent; increase

G. affluence _____

7. v. to regard with extreme hatred; detest utterly; loathe

H. alleviate _____

8. adj. of keen penetration or discernment; insightful

I. aloof _____

9. adj. of warlike character; aggressively hostile; bellicose

J. ambivalence _____ 10. v. to comply; submit

K. amiable _____ 11. n. a coming into place, view, or being; arrival

L. apathy _____ 12. v. to make easier to endure; lessen in severity

M. archaic _____ 13. n. uncertainty or fluctuation, esp. when caused by inability to make a choice

N. assiduous _____ 14. adv. at a distance, esp. in feeling or interest; apart; adj. reserved; indifferent

O. astute _____ 15. v. to free from guilt or blame or their consequences

P. attribute _____ 16. adj. constant; unremitting; hard-working

Q. augment _____ 17. n. absence or suppression of passion, emotion, or excitement

R. aversion _____ 18. n. abundance of money, property, and other material goods; riches; wealth

S. banal _____ 19. adj. marked by the characteristics of an earlier period

T. belligerent _____ 20. v. to approach and speak to aggressively

300pts

100pts

Week 2

cede

convex

"Learning is not attained by chance.
It must be sought for with ardor and
attended to with diligence."
- Abigail Adams

verb

adj.

Start   Restart

1.

beneficent *adj.*

characterized by or performing acts of kindness or charity

Her beneficent deeds brought joy to the downtrodden in her community.

2.

benevolence *n.*

desire to do good to others; goodwill; charitableness

The wizard was frequently noted for his benevolence in granting wishes to all who came to him.

3.

benign *adj.*

harmless; having little or no detrimental effect; having a kindly disposition; gracious

Martha was relieved when the doctor determined that her tumor was a benign form of cancer.

4.

berate *v.*

to scold; to use abusive language

It is rude to berate someone just because they don't appear to be as smart as you are.

5.

bereave *v.*

to deprive and make desolate, esp. by death

We wept, bereaved of our great aunt, who had been an inspiration to us all.

6.

beset *v.*

to attack on all sides

Ever since he had moved to Philadelphia, he had been beset with problems.

7.

bewilder *v.*

to confuse or puzzle completely; perplex

I was bewildered by your comment: do you really believe you see a spirit hovering around me?

8.

blaspheme *v.*

to speak impiously or irreverently of (God or sacred things)

When he shook his fist in the air, many interpreted his act as one in which he blasphemed God for taking away his young child.

WEEK 1
WEEK 2
WEEK 3
WEEK 4
WEEK 5
WEEK 6
WEEK 7
WEEK 8
WEEK 9
WEEK 10
REGULAR

9.

blazon   v.

to set forth openly; display; proclaim

The newspaper blazoned across the front page that the national championship had been won by the local high school.

10.

blithe   adj.

joyous, merry, or gay in disposition; carefree

Weddings and births are blithe occasions.

11.

bombastic   adj.

using pompous, noisy, and arrogant language

College freshmen newly introduced to controversial ideas often become bombastic when they start to express their newfound beliefs.

12.

boor   n.

arrogant, rude or unmannered person

The horrible house guest with the bad attitude was such a boor; I will now see him as a boar.

13.

brandish   v.

to shake or wave, as a weapon; flourish

The three musketeers brandished their swords against the corrupt Marquis.

14.

breadth   n.

width; range or scope

The breadth of knowledge of most professors at major universities is amazing.

15.

bridle   n.

a harness fitted around a horse's head to guide the animal; (v.) to control or restrain

The young rider saw that the young horse was still so spirited that he had to keep it under control by placing a bridle in its mouth.

16.

brusque   adj.

abrupt in manner; blunt; rough

Agnes often intimidated her students whenever she answered their questions in a brusque manner.

17.

bungle

v.

to do in a clumsy, incompetent, or unsuccessful manner

Danny and David were caught after they had bungled the robbery of the bank.

18.

buoyant

adj.

cheering or invigorating; tending to float in a fluid;

The gentle breeze, the warm sun, and the picnic atmosphere put Harvey in a buoyant and festive mood.

19.

buttress

v.

to support or reinforce

The author buttressed her analysis with lengthy dissections of several of Moore's poems.

20.

bygone

adj.

from ages past

She yearned for bygone eras when chivalry still existed and men actually opened doors for ladies.

21.

cacophony

n.

a disagreeable, harsh, or discordant sound or combination of sounds or tones

The cacophony of the children's orchestra drove their parents into the backyard.

22.

cajole

v.

to persuade by flattery or promises; coax

Pete's friends cajoled him to remain at the party even though he was no longer in the mood to have fun.

23.

camaraderie

n.

association of friendship within any group or organization

We experienced a great deal of camaraderie while we were at summer camp and made many close friends.

24.

candor

n.

the state or quality of being frank, open, and sincere in speech or expression

Let me speak with you with candor, not hiding what you need to know: the truth.

WEEK 1
WEEK 2
WEEK 3
WEEK 4
WEEK 5
WEEK 6
WEEK 7
WEEK 8
WEEK 9
WEEK 10

REGULAR

25.

cantankerous   adj.

disagreeable to deal with; contentious

Old Mr. Briggs was a cantankerous man, screaming at birds that woke him in the morning.

26.

canvass   v.

to solicit votes, opinions, or orders; investigate

Carrying his clipboard and stack of surveys, the pollster canvassed the neighborhood, asking questions door to door.

27.

caprice   n.

a sudden, unpredictable change, as of one's mind or the weather

Ethel has given into her whim, to satisfy her momentary caprice.

28.

caricature   n.

a picture, description, etc., ludicrously exaggerating the peculiarities or defects of persons or things

The caricature of the President was instantly recognizable because the artist had exaggerated his most distinctive features.

29.

carnage   n.

massacre

News programs showed footage of the carnage, eliciting global sympathy for the rebels who were so brutally killed.

30.

carnal   adj.

sensual; relating to physical appetites

The town had a reputation as a center of carnal pleasure, not a place for those of strong moral and religious faith.

31.

cede   v.

to pass a title to

The king ceded his throne to his son when he thought the son was old enough for the responsibility.

32.

celestial   adj.

relating to the heavens or universe

The astronomer hopes to discover a celestial body and name it after himself.

33.

censure

n.

strong or vehement expression of disapproval; (v.) to criticize in a harsh or strong manner

Andrew Jackson received a strong censure from the Senate for his anti-bank policies in the 1830s.

34.

chagrin

n.

keen annoyance, or shock, as at one's failures or errors

To my chagrin, I discovered I had bought too little caviar for the party.

35.

chary

adj.

very cautious, careful

One should always be chary of the risks involved in bungee jumping.

36.

chasm

n.

a yawning hollow, as in the earth's surface; great and deep expanse

The meteor smashing into the Earth's surface created a chasm nearly half a mile wide and two miles deep.

37.

chaste

adj.

morally pure; virginal

In ancient times, young girls were expected to live a chaste life without dating any boys.

38.

chasten

v.

to inflict suffering upon for purposes of moral improvement; chastise

The sacrificial maiden was chastened for not being chaste.

39.

chastise

v.

to criticize severely; to discipline

Relief organizations have chastised the government for not doing enough to alleviate world hunger.

40.

chide

v.

to express disapproval of; scold

His mother gently chided the naughty child for speaking too loudly in the museum.

WEEK 1
WEEK 2
WEEK 3
WEEK 4
WEEK 5
WEEK 6
WEEK 7
WEEK 8
WEEK 9
WEEK 10

REGULAR

41.

christen

v.

to name in baptism; name and dedicate

The new parents christened their baby "Mary" after the Virgin Mary.

42.

chronic

adj.

habitual or prolonged period

After being a chronic smoker for twenty years, she was at great risk for lung cancer.

43.

cipher

v.

to put in secret writing; encode

The government ciphered many of their wartime messages so that the enemy could not read them.

44.

circumscribe

v.

to limit or restrict, often by establishing certain boundaries; to draw a line around; encircle

The cook knew that the likes and dislikes of his customers would circumscribe his freedom to cook whatever he wished.

45.

circumspect

adj.

watchful and discreet; cautious; prudent

The circumspect hunter looked around for possible traps before proceeding with caution.

46.

civility

n.

courtesy; politeness

Edwina was respected for acting with civility when confronting the rowdy protestors at the City council meeting.

47.

clamorous

adj.

marked by loud outcry; urgent in complaint or demand.

Hearing the clamorous noise emitting from his classroom, the teacher raced back to investigate.

48.

clandestine

adj.

characterized by, done in, or executed with secrecy or concealment, esp. for purposes of subversion or deception

The old man used a candle to light his way up the clandestine stairway.

49.

clemency
n.

disposition to show compassion, or forgiveness in judging or punishing; merciful

The King showed such unusual clemency that all the noblemen of the court were shocked when he let the bandits leave without punishment.

50.

coax
v.

to attempt to influence by gentle persuasion, flattery

How could I coax you into doing some of the work I have to do?

51.

coddle
v.

to treat tenderly; nurse or tend indulgently; pamper

The little boy was coddled by both sets of grandparents, so he got used to being pampered.

52.

cohesive
adj.

having the property of consistency

Despite all her training in rhetoric, Jane felt herself unable to maintain a cohesive argument.

53.

cohort
n.

a group or company

Maggie's cohort, her friends and classmates, attended her graduation.

54.

collaborate
v.

to work, one with another; cooperate, as on a literary work

It is the goal of all the cities in the county to collaborate on road improvements.

55.

colloquial
adj.

pertaining or peculiar to common speech as distinguished from literary

When I read her letter, it felt as though I were talking to her, since she liked to write in a colloquial style.

56.

combustible
adj.

capable of catching fire; flammable

Because of gasoline's highly combustible property, smoking is prohibited at all gas stations.

WEEK 1
WEEK 2
WEEK 3
WEEK 4
WEEK 5
WEEK 6
WEEK 7
WEEK 8
WEEK 9
WEEK 10

REGULAR

57.

comely
adj.

pleasing in appearance; attractive; fair

The comely young lady was very popular among the men; her homely sister, however, was not.

58.

commodity
n.

something that is bought and sold

While the ocean may be a beautiful wonderland to most, to the fishing industry it is nothing but a commodity to be plundered for profit.

59.

commune
v.

to converse or talk together, usually with profound intensity, intimacy, etc.; interchange thoughts or feelings

Let us commune together, with a dinner, to cement our growing friendship.

60.

commute
v.

to put something, especially something less severe, in place of; to travel some distance between home and one's place of work

The judge, out of the kindness of his heart, decided to commute the lifetime sentence into a 25-year sentence.

61.

complacent
adj.

pleased, esp. with oneself or one's merits, advantages or situations, often without awareness of some potential danger or defect; self-satisfied

Great success should not make one complacent, but rather have a humbling effect.

62.

complement
v.

to complete or match; (n.) something that completes or makes perfect

I have to say that your orange and purple spotted shoes do not complement the rest of your dark suit.

63.

complicity
n.

participation or partnership, as in wrong-doing or with a wrong-doer

The suspect tried to deny his complicity in the crime.

64.

comport
v.

to conduct (oneself); behave

You must comport yourself properly at this school, since it has a history of attracting the highest class of students.

65.

composure   n.

calmness

The tellers showed composure during the bank robbery, even while everybody else was screaming.

66.

compress   v.

to squeeze together or compact in less space; condense

Don't try to compress an entire essay into just a few sentences if you need to explain in more detail what you mean.

67.

conciliate   v.

to overcome the distrust or hostility of; placate; win over

They would sit together, getting rid of their fears, to conciliate, working out their problems toward a practical solution.

68.

concoct   v.

prepare by mixing ingredients

The bartender concocted a fancy drink consisting of at least twelve ingredients.

69.

concord   n.

harmony

The key to concord and happy living is acting respectfully of others and making sacrifices when necessary.

70.

concur   v.

to accord in opinion; agree

I concur with his evaluation that the city needs a new energy source besides the power plant across the county line.

71.

condemn   v.

to express an unfavorable or adverse judgment on; indicate strong disapproval of; censure

He condemned the policies that seemed to support torture of prisoners.

72.

condescending   adj.

showing or implying a usually patronizing descent from dignity or superiority

The young heiress treated the servants in such a condescending way that many of them are plotting to put cat hair in her soup.

WEEK 1
WEEK 2
WEEK 3
WEEK 4
WEEK 5
WEEK 6
WEEK 7
WEEK 8
WEEK 9
WEEK 10

REGULAR

73.

condolence n.

expression of sympathy with a person who is suffering sorrow, misfortune, or grief

I want to send my condolences at the death of your grandfather yesterday.

74.

conduit n.

a means for transporting something, particularly a tube, pipe, or passageway for a fluid

The waterway served as a conduit for the waste products flowing out of the city.

75.

confederate n.

a person, group, nation, etc., united with others in a confederacy; an ally; (adj.) united in a league, alliance, or conspiracy; (v.) to unite in a league, alliance, or conspiracy

The small island country sought through a skillful diplomacy to become a confederate of its neighbors.

76.

confounded adj.

bewildered; confused; perplexed

Henrietta was confounded by the math problem regarding compounding interested.

77.

confute v.

to prove to be false, invalid, or defective; disprove

Lenny could not confute the assertion by his best friend that Lenny could never use a sentence without using the word 'like.'

78.

congenial adj.

agreeable, suitable, or pleasing in nature or character

The hosts were very congenial to their guests, taking their coats and escorting them into the party.

79.

congregate v.

to bring together into a crowd

Students congregated in the quad to protest the firing of their favorite teacher.

80.

connive v.

to act in a secretive manner

The thieves connived for many months to figure out a way to rob the local bank.

81.

conscientious adj.

controlled by or done according to conscience

The conscientious teenager truly wanted to do good in the world, so none of us were surprised when she joined the Peace Corps.

82.

consecrate v.

to set apart as sacred

The Pope consecrated the new structure, designating it as a religious spot of special significance.

83.

consensus n.

a collective unanimous opinion of a number of persons

The general consensus of the members of the club was that our president was not doing his job very well, so we decided to hold a special election.

84.

conspicuous adj.

easily seen or noticed; readily visible or observable

The engagement ring was very conspicuous, a large, pale pink Harry Winston diamond.

85.

consternation n.

panic, mental anguish

A wave of consternation passed among the wedding guests when they learned that the groom snuck out the back with a mysterious woman.

86.

constituent n.

one who has the right to vote at an election

The constituent wrote to her assemblyman to request his presence at the high school graduation.

87.

constrict v.

to bind

We tried to tie a string around the bag to constrict the opening, but the beans spilled out anyway.

88.

contagion n.

the communication of disease from person to person

The contagion spread through the office, so that by the end of the Christmas holidays, everyone was ill.

WEEK 1
WEEK 2
WEEK 3
WEEK 4
WEEK 5
WEEK 6
WEEK 7
WEEK 8
WEEK 9
WEEK 10
REGULAR

89.

contemplate v.

to consider thoughtfully

At some point in life, it is natural to begin to contemplate the meaning of existence.

90.

contemporaneous adj.

living, occurring, or existing at the same time

Shakespeare's plays must be understood as contemporaneous with lifestyles in Elizabethan England.

91.

contemptible adj.

worthy of scorn or disdain

The contemptible criminal stood in front of the judge and lied, saying he felt remorse for all the damage he had done.

92.

contend v.

to strive in opposition, compete in a race; debate

Several young men contended for the few spots on the Olympic track and field team.

93.

contentious adj.

tending to argument or strife; quarrelsome

Michelle was contentious, arguing with her workers over who would make the coffee and who would close the file cabinets at the end of the day.

94.

contrite adj.

caused by or showing sincere remorse

The guilty little boy actually looked contrite when we ordered him to stand in the corner facing the wall, but that was probably because he hated that punishment.

95.

contrive v.

to manage or carry through by some device or scheme

We contrived a new sales strategy that resulted in our selling three times as much as we had in the past month.

96.

conundrum n.

a riddle, the answer to which involves a pun or play on words

The advanced sudoku puzzle was a conundrum; no solution seemed to fit the given arrangement of numbers.

97.

convene   v.

to summon or cause to assemble

The committee called the members to convene at the convention center.

98.

converge   v.

to cause to incline and approach nearer together

Where the land became less populated, the roads converged into one.

99.

convex   adj.

having a surface or boundary that curves outward

The gilded surface of the convex dome glittered in the sun.

100.

convey   v.

to communicate; impart; make known

He wished to convey his sympathies to the family for the loss of their youngest child.

WEEK **1**

WEEK **2**

WEEK **3**

WEEK **4**

WEEK **5**

WEEK **6**

WEEK **7**

WEEK **8**

WEEK **9**

WEEK **10**

A. Fill in the appropriate words using the clues below.

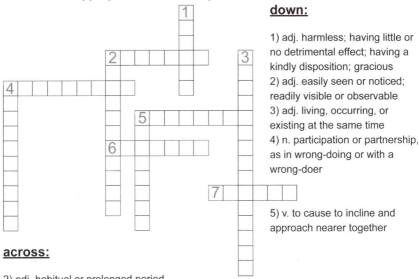

down:

1) adj. harmless; having little or no detrimental effect; having a kindly disposition; gracious
2) adj. easily seen or noticed; readily visible or observable
3) adj. living, occurring, or existing at the same time
4) n. participation or partnership, as in wrong-doing or with a wrong-doer

5) v. to cause to incline and approach nearer together

across:

2) adj. habitual or prolonged period
4) n. a disagreeable, harsh, or discordant sound or combination of sounds or tones
5) adj. having the property of consistency
6) v. to act in a secretive manner
7) adj. morally pure; virginal

B. Match the words on the left with their appropriate definitions on the right.

A. benevolence _____

B. berate _____

C. bombastic _____

D. brusque _____

E. camaraderie _____

F. candor _____

G. cantankerous _____

H. chagrin _____

I. cipher _____

J. circumspect _____

K. clandestine _____

L. colloquial _____

M. complacent _____

N. conciliate _____

O. concur _____

P. condescending _____

Q. consecrate _____

R. contemplate _____

S. contend _____

T. contrive _____

1. v. to put in secret writing; encode

2. v. to accord in opinion; agree

3. adj. using pompous, noisy, and arrogant language

4. v. to strive in opposition, compete in a race; debate

5. v. to scold; to use abusive language

6. adj. characterized by, done in, or executed with secrecy or concealment

7. adj. pleased, esp. with oneself or one's merits, advantages, situation; self-satisfied

8. n. desire to do good to others; goodwill; charitableness

9. v. to overcome the distrust or hostility of; placate; win over

10. adj. abrupt in manner; blunt; rough

11. adj. disagreeable to deal with; contentious

12. n. the state or quality of being frank, open, and sincere in speech or expression

13. v. to manage or carry through by some device or scheme

14. n. association of friendship within any group or organization

15. adj. pertaining or peculiar to common speech as distinguished from literary

16. adj. showing or implying a usually patronizing descent from dignity or superiority

17. v. to consider thoughtfully

18. n. keen annoyance, as at one's failures or errors

19. adj. watchful and discreet; cautious; prudent

20. v. to set apart as sacred

300pts

100pts

Week 3

curt

derision

"Develop a passion for learning.
If you do, you will never cease to grow."
- Anthony J. D'Angelo,
The College Blue Book

adj.

noun

Start   Restart

1.

convivial   adj.

friendly; agreeable

There is no place for gloom at such convivial settings such as graduations or weddings.

2.

convoluted   adj.

complicated; intricately involved

The teacher shook her head in disbelief as she listened to the student's convoluted excuse for his missing homework.

3.

convulsion   n.

a violent and abnormal muscular contraction of the body

The patient underwent several convulsions before becoming still.

4.

copious   adj.

large in quantity or number; abundant; plentiful

Jill earned extra cash by taking copious notes in all her classes and selling them to fellow students.

5.

cordial   adj.

courteous and gracious; friendly; warm

Jessica is such a cordial host that I always look forward to attending her parties.

6.

corpulent   adj.

large or bulky of body; portly; stout; fat

Four pizzas a day will make even the most slender of individuals rather corpulent.

7.

correlative   adj.

mutually involving or implying one another

The correlative relationship between exercise and obesity is inverse: the more one exercises, the less likely one is to be obese.

8.

correspond   v.

to be in agreement or conformity

The rise in crime often corresponds to the lack of job opportunities for young men in the city.

9.

corroborate v.

to strengthen, as proof or conviction

Hugo was able to corroborate Mel's findings and secure widespread support for Mel's new theory of quantum movement.

10.

covenant n.

an agreement entered into by two or more persons or parties

The new tenants signed a covenant which dictated how often they were required to mow the lawn.

11.

covert adj.

concealed; secret; disguised; (n.) a covering; cover

Soldiers in covert operations kidnapped the President without anyone's knowledge.

12.

covetous adj.

excessively or wrongly desirous of wealth or possessions; greedy

She was jealous of her friend's success and covetous of his possessions.

13.

credence n.

belief as to the truth of something

Putting a telephone in Lincoln's office in the White House obviously diminished the credence of the movie that it was an accurate historical reflection of the Civil War era.

14.

crystallize v.

to bring together or give fixed shape to

Although the idea had not crystallized in Trevor's mind, he began to take notes in order to find direction.

15.

culminate v.

reach an expected conclusion

The 4th of July celebration culminates in a fantastic display of fireworks.

16.

culpable adj.

guilty

The culpable girl looked appropriately remorseful, and we all forgave her because she was so cute.

WEEK 1
WEEK 2
WEEK 3
WEEK 4
WEEK 5
WEEK 6
WEEK 7
WEEK 8
WEEK 9
WEEK 10

REGULAR

17.

cursory   adj.

going rapidly over something, without noticing details; hasty; superficial

He went over the contract in a cursory manner since he had already negotiated the terms with his lawyer.

18.

curt   adj.

concise, compressed, and abrupt in act or expression

The employee at Tiffany's was curt at best when answering my questions, presumably because I didn't look like I was the type to buy anything there.

19.

curtail   v.

to cut short; cut off a part of; reduce; diminish

They decided to curtail the meeting when it was discovered that the room was to be fumigated.

20.

cynical   adj.

like or characteristic of a cynic; distrusting or mocking the motives of others

Alexis was cynical, never trusting people no matter how kind they were to her.

21.

dastardly   adj.

cowardly; meanly base; sneaking

The man called the senator dastardly for not standing up for his beliefs during the debate, but merely attacking his opponent's tragic family upbringing.

22.

dauntless   adj.

not to be intimidated; fearless; bold

The dauntless Hollywood stuntman jumped into the flaming buildling and came crashing out through the window.

23.

debase   v.

to reduce in quality or value

They debased the purity of the gold with some weak alloys.

24.

debauch   v.

to seduce; to corrupt by sensuality, intemperance; (n.) a period of sensual self-indulgence

Drunkenness was only one of the ways that the fraternity boys debauched themselves on the weekend.

25.

debunk
v.

show to be false

It is necessary for parents to debunk the advertising claims that entice their youngsters with empty promises of fun.

26.

decamp
v.

to leave suddenly or unexpectedly

The soldiers were ordered to decamp in the middle of the night so as to sneak up on the enemy.

27.

decipher
v.

to find out the true words or meaning of, as something hardly legible

Scholars today still can't decipher certain hieroglyphic symbols that the Egyptians used.

28.

decorum
n.

dignified propriety of behavior, speech, dress, etc.

Every person in the banquet acted with the highest grace and decorum.

29.

decoy
n.

anything that allures, or is intended to allure into danger or temptation

The first plane was a decoy to throw off the enemy; the President was actually in the second plane.

30.

decrepit
adj.

enfeebled, as by old age or some chronic infirmity

Prince John accused the aging king of becoming decrepit and demanded to be crowned as the new king.

31.

deface
v.

to mar the surface or appearance of; disfigure

Graffiti is not art, but rather vandalism that defaces private property.

32.

defame
v.

to slander

Thinking that the journalists had defamed him in the morning paper, the manager initiated a lawsuit against them.

WEEK 1
WEEK 2
WEEK 3
WEEK 4
WEEK 5
WEEK 6
WEEK 7
WEEK 8
WEEK 9
WEEK 10

REGULAR

33.

default   v.

to fail to do what is required; to fail to pay, esp. on a loan

Chuck worried that if he could not find a better paying job, he might have to default on his student loans.

34.

deference   n.

respectful submission or yielding, as to another's opinion, wishes, or judgment

The husband showed deference to his wife's last wishes and carried out her will exactly as she intended.

35.

defraud   v.

to deprive of a right, money, or property by fraud

An internet scam can unwittingly defraud you of hundreds, if not thousands of dollars.

36.

defray   v.

to bear or pay all or part of (the costs, expenses, etc.)

We would defray the cost of shipping if you buy our books in bulk.

37.

deft   adj.

dexterous; nimble; skillful; clever

Kim was deft on the piano, handling the complicated Chopin piece with flair.

38.

defunct   adj.

no longer in use

The now defunct nuclear plant is being used as a storage facility for waste.

39.

degenerate   v.

to become worse or inferior

The handsome young man's life degenerated when he turned to drugs and alcohol.

40.

degrade   v.

to take away honors or position from

The lieutenant degraded the soldier in the presence of others and made him turn red with shame.

41.

deify
v.

to regard or worship as a god

As we are all human, none of us can rightly be deified.

42.

deity
n.

a god or goddess

As opposed to the monotheistic religions of the West, believing only in one god, many Eastern religions have several deities.

43.

deject
v.

to dishearten

After another humiliating loss, the team felt dejected, but they soon realized that they would be foolish simply to give up.

44.

deleterious
adj.

hurtful, morally or physically

The surgeon general frequently issues warnings about the deleterious effects of smoking.

45.

delineate
v.

to represent by sketch or diagram

Without a map, the trail guide delineated the route to the hidden waterfall using sticks and rocks on the bare ground.

46.

delusion
n.

a false belief which is strongly held despite contrary evidence

Many people who suffer from mental illness experience delusions of persecution, believing everyone is against them.

47.

demean
v.

to lower in dignity, honor, or standing; debase

You should not demean any group with whom you may work over the next several years.

48.

demeanor
n.

the way in which a person behaves

Although her demeanor was gruff, she was very sympathetic.

WEEK 1
WEEK 2
WEEK 3
WEEK 4
WEEK 5
WEEK 6
WEEK 7
WEEK 8
WEEK 9
WEEK 10

REGULAR

49.

demise

n.

death; the time when something ends; the eventual failure of something previously successful

Mr. Gibson's racist comment ultimately led to the demise of his career.

50.

demobilize

v.

to disband, as troops

The Japanese army was demobilized immediately after losing World War II.

51.

demote

v.

lower in position or rank

Father was despondent when he was demoted from manager to clerk.

52.

demure

adj.

characterized by shyness and modesty; reserved

The demure young girl was so quiet during the party that few people even realized her presence.

53.

denigrate

v.

to speak damagingly of; criticize in a derogatory manner; defame

He denigrated his boss over the internet by posting scandalous rumors on his blog.

54.

dense

adj.

slow-witted; dull; difficult to understand or follow because of being closely packed with ideas or complexities of style

Horace was not the brightest guy in the class; in fact, he was too dense to realize when he had been insulted.

55.

deplore

v.

to regret deeply or strongly; lament

Mr. Thomas deplored how so few of the graduating students actually enrolled in universities.

56.

deploy

v.

send out on a stated mission

Countless platoons have been deployed to Iraq since the inception of the war on terrorism.

57.

deport v.

to take or send away forcibly, as to a penal colony

The illegal immigrant was deported back to his country by the U.S. government.

58.

depose v.

remove from a place of authority

The revolutionaries deposed the cruel dictator, ushering in democratic government.

59.

depository n.

a place where anything is kept in safety

The government safe served as a depository for top secret documents.

60.

depravity n.

moral corruption or degradation

One of the many reasons believed by historians that contributed to Rome's fall was its moral depravity.

61.

depreciate v.

to lessen the value or price of

The vase depreciated in value because it was discovered not to be made by the famous potter.

62.

derelict adj.

neglectful of obligation

The derelict apartment was unfurnished, run down, and generally unsuitable to live in.

63.

derision n.

ridicule

The awful performance elicited cries of derision from the audience.

64.

derisive adj.

scornful, mocking, contemptible

The mean boy's derisive comment about the girl's new hairdo made the girl cry.

WEEK 1
WEEK 2
WEEK 3
WEEK 4
WEEK 5
WEEK 6
WEEK 7
WEEK 8
WEEK 9
WEEK 10

REGULAR

65.

derogatory

adj.

disparaging; speaking ill of

After enduring his derogatory comments for an hour, Clarissa finally tried to defend herself against John's attack.

66.

despondent

adj.

downcast or disheartened; lacking hope or courage

Do not be so despondent or give way to a life of sorrow because of the loss of one love.

67.

despot

n.

an absolute and irresponsible monarch

The despot quelled rebellions with absolute force and tolerated no dissent in his government.

68.

destitute

adj.

without means of subsistence; lacking food, clothing, and shelter

The former investment banker was now destitute, having lost all his assets in the stock market crash.

69.

detract

v.

to take away in such manner as to lessen value or estimation

The huge tattoo of a pit bull on the woman's arm detracted from her beautiful face.

70.

detrimental

adj.

damaging; harmful

Cigarette smoking has been known for generations to be detrimental to one's health.

71.

deviate

v.

to take a different course

We deviated from the planned course of our road trip to take a spontaneous detour to see some historical landmarks.

72.

dexterous

adj.

skillful or adroit in the use of the hands or body

No matter how old he got, Mr. Plato was dexterous in both body and mind, able to do 50 sit ups and read the *New York Times* cover to cover.

73.

dialect n.

variety of a language that is distinguished from other varieties of the same language by features of grammar, and vocabulary, and by its use by a group of speakers who are set off from others geographically or socially

The family spoke a little known dialect exclusive to the region.

74.

differentiate v.

to form or mark differently from other such things; distinguish

The school district did an excellent job differentiating between students who were capable of handling AP work and those who were not.

75.

diffident adj.

lacking confidence in one's own ability, worth, or fitness; timid; shy

She remained diffident, unsure whether or not she could perform her tasks well.

76.

diffusion n.

the act of spreading or extending widely

The diffusion of knowledge in ancient times was a slow, unreliable process.

77.

digress v.

to turn aside from the main subject and for a time dwell on some incidental matter

The professor often digressed during his lectures, but because his stories were so interesting, his students didn't mind.

78.

dilapidated adj.

fallen into decay or partial ruin

The dilapidated old hut has clearly been abandoned for many years.

79.

dilate v.

to make wider or larger; to cause to expand

When I went to get my eyes checked, the optometrist dilated my pupils so that he could see into them more clearly.

80.

diminutive adj.

small; little; tiny

The talented seven-year old basketball player still made a diminutive figure among teens he played the game with.

WEEK 1

WEEK 2

WEEK 3

WEEK 4

WEEK 5

WEEK 6

WEEK 7

WEEK 8

WEEK 9

WEEK 10

REGULAR

81.

din
n.

loud, confused noise

The rowdy tavern patrons created a great din with their uproarious singing.

82.

dire
adj.

causing great fear or suffering

The dire situation gave the President no time to dawdle; he had to make a decision immediately or risk the outbreak of war.

83.

disavow
v.

to disclaim knowledge of, connection with, or responsibility for; disown

She refused to disavow her associations with her brother-in-law, who had swindled the family of thousands of dollars.

84.

discharge
v.

dismiss, fire; unload or relieve of a load

Three weeks after being admitted into the hospital, I was discharged with stern instructions to take it easy for a while.

85.

disciple
n.

one who believes the teaching of another, or who adopts and follows some doctrine

After he proposed his theory of time travel, Professor Lund attracted a following of disciples dedicated to proving it.

86.

disconcert
v.

trouble, disturb

They looked at each other dumbly, apparently disconcerted by the stunning new revelations.

87.

disconsolate
adj.

unable to be comforted; hopelessly unhappy; inconsolable

The disconsolate mother, still unable to come to terms with his death, decided not to go to her son's funeral.

88.

discord
n.

absence of harmoniousness

Frequent discord between mother and father negatively affects children's emotional development.

89.

discredit   v.

to injure the credit or reputation of; (n.) loss or lack of belief or confidence; disbelief; distrust

He was discredited by his frequent lies; no one would ever buy anything from him at his store because of the countless times he went back on a deal.

90.

discrepancy   n.

inconsistency

The discrepancy between the two witnesses' accounts led the prosecutor to believe that one of them was lying.

91.

discriminate   v.

to make a distinction in favor of or against a person or thing on the basis of the group, class, or category to which the person or thing belongs rather than according to actual merit; show partiality

Expert wine drinkers can discriminate between the finest of wines and most brands which they deem mediocre.

92.

discursive   adj.

passing aimlessly from one subject to another; rambling

In meditation one closely observes his or her discursive mind.

93.

disdain   v.

to look upon or treat with contempt; despise

John held Katie in disdain for having hurt his best friend David.

94.

disinterested   adj.

unbiased by personal interest or advantage; not influenced by selfish motives

The judge was remarkably disinterested and spent a long time listening to our stories before coming to a fair verdict.

95.

dismount   v.

to throw down, push off, or otherwise remove from a horse or the like

The jockey dismounted his famous horse after winning the Kentucky Derby and pumped his fist in the air.

96.

disparage   v.

to regard or speak of slightingly

Do not disparage your parents for trying to bring some discipline to your life.

WEEK 1
WEEK 2
WEEK 3
WEEK 4
WEEK 5
WEEK 6
WEEK 7
WEEK 8
WEEK 9
WEEK 10

REGULAR

97.

dispassionate adj.

free from or unaffected by passion;
devoid of personal feeling or bias;
impartial

The author's dispassionate voice and unattractive looks belied his ardent nature.

98.

dispense v.

to deal out in portions; distribute

The free medical clinic dispensed mild cold remedies and bandages to assist with the poor community.

99.

disposition n.

the predominant or prevailing tendency of
one's spirits; natural mental and emotional
outlook or mood; characteristic attitude;
physical inclination or tendency

Annie's disposition often embarrasses others because she cannot appear in public without being verbally disruptive.

100.

dissemble v.

to hide by pretending something
different

Tom dissembled that he was ill when in fact he was just bored and wanted to play hooky.

A. Fill in the appropriate words using the clues below.

across:

2) v. to seduce; to corrupt by sensuality, intemperance; (n.) a period of sensual self-indulgence

5) adj. neglectful of obligation

6) n. respectful submission or yielding, as to another's opinion, wishes, or judgment

7) adj. passing aimlessly from one subject to another; rambling

8) adj. hurtful, morally or physically

down:

1) v. reach an expected conclusion

3) adj. complicated; intricately involved

4) v. to regret deeply or strongly; lament

5) adj. small; little; tiny

6) adj. no longer in use

B. Match the words on the left with their appropriate definitions on the right.

A. copious _____ 1. n. inconsistency

B. corroborate _____ 2. adj. like or characteristic of a cynic; distrusting or mocking the motives of others

C. covert _____ 3. n. moral corruption or degradation

D. culpable _____ 4. adj. damaging; harmful

E. cynical _____ 5. adj. concealed; secret; disguised.; n. a covering; cover

F. decorum _____ 6. adj. enfeebled, as by old age or some chronic infirmity

G. decrepit _____ 7. adj. characterized by shyness and modesty; reserved

H. delineate _____ 8. v. to make wider or larger; to cause to expand

I. demeanor _____ 9. v. to represent by sketch or diagram

J. demure _____ 10. n. dignified propriety of behavior, speech, dress, etc.

K. depravity _____ 11. n. the way in which a person behaves

L. derogatory _____ 12. adj. skillful or adroit in the use of the hands or body

M. despot _____ 13. v. to strengthen, as proof or conviction

N. detrimental _____ 14. adj. disparaging; speaking ill of

O. deviate _____ 15. v. to take a different course

P. dexterous _____ 16. n. an absolute and irresponsible monarch

Q. dilate _____ 17. adj. guilty

R. dire _____ 18. v. to regard or speak of slightingly

S. discrepancy _____ 19. adj. large in quantity or number; abundant; plentiful

T. disparage _____ 20. adj. causing great fear or suffering

300pts

100pts

Week 4

emit

enmity

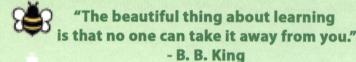
"The beautiful thing about learning
is that no one can take it away from you."
- B. B. King

verb

noun

1.

disseminate   v.

to scatter or spread widely, as though sowing seed; promulgate extensively; broadcast; disperse

The Nazis disseminated wartime propaganda in the form of posters, radio broadcasts, and newspaper ads.

2.

dissipate   v.

to disperse or disappear

The scent of the perfume we sprayed into the air quickly dissipated.

3.

dissolute   adj.

lacking moral restraint; indulging in sensual pleasures or vices

The dissolute young man was ruined because of his wish for instant gratification.

4.

dissonance   n.

harsh or disagreeable sound

The dissonance of the schoolyard at recess disturbed Freda's afternoon nap.

5.

distemper   n.

a disease or malady

He died of a broken heart, a distemper which kills many more than is generally supposed.

6.

distill   v.

to extract or produce by vaporization and condensation

We distilled the mountain spring water in order to make it drinkable.

7.

distort   v.

to twist into an unnatural or irregular form

The conspiracy theorists distorted the truth, saying the government had engineered a huge cover-up.

8.

distraught   adj.

bewildered

The distraught mother of the kidnapping victim cried uncontrollably for days.

WEEK 1
WEEK 2
WEEK 3
WEEK 4
WEEK 5
WEEK 6
WEEK 7
WEEK 8
WEEK 9
WEEK 10

REGULAR

9.
divergent
adj.

tending in different directions

Because of the liberal atmosphere in my family, it is acceptable to express a divergent opinion during heated political discussions.

10.
divest
v.

to strip, specifically of ceremonial clothes, ornaments, or military equipment

The soldiers divested the prisoners of all their assets before they were locked up.

11.
docile
adj.

easy to manage

The girl was so docile that we frequently compared her to a little lamb, always taking orders and never giving them.

12.
dogged
adj.

persistent in effort; stubbornly tenacious

The dogged lawyer is nicknamed "The Pitbull" because once he gets a case, he never gives up until he wins.

13.
dogmatic
adj.

making statements, often arrogantly, without argument or evidence

The new priest at our church is so dogmatic that parishioners are beginning to abandon the congregation.

14.
doleful
adj.

sorrowful; mournful

The black and white picture of the rural funeral procession emphasizes the doleful mood of the occasion.

15.
domineer
v.

to rule over or control someone in an arbitrary, cruel, or tyrannical way

The husband domineered over his wife for many years before she finally got sick of it and filed for divorce.

16.
dubious
adj.

doubtful

Because her story was rather dubious, the police held Joan for further questioning.

.

17.

ductile

adj.

capable of being drawn out, as into wire or a thread

The electrician unrolled the ball of ductile copper for his wires.

18.

duplicity

n.

deceitfulness in speech or conduct; speaking or acting in two different ways concerning the same matter with intent to deceive; double-dealing

Shocked by the spies' duplicity, the President recommended that they be executed for crimes against the state.

19.

earnest

adj.

having or showing deep sincerity or seriousness

Your earnest expression of interest in nature has convinced me to buy you the science kit you asked for.

20.

ebullient

adj.

overflowing with fervor, enthusiasm, or excitement; high-spirited

The Mexican embassy greeted the visiting President with an ebullient reception.

21.

eccentric

adj.

deviating from the recognized or customary character, practice, etc.; irregular; erratic; peculiar; odd; (n.) a person who has an unusual, peculiar, or odd personality, set of beliefs, or behavior pattern

Mrs. McCann was quite eccentric; she liked using a leash to walk her three cats.

22.

ecstatic

adj.

joyful

When the last number of the lottery was read, Fred was ecstatic, for he had just won $10,000.

23.

edict

n.

a decree issued by a sovereign or other authority

The church issued an edict prohibiting all dancing and singing on the premise.

24.

edify

v.

to build up, or strengthen, especially in morals or religion

This course is intended to edify those curious about Enlightenment.

WEEK 1
WEEK 2
WEEK 3
WEEK 4
WEEK 5
WEEK 6
WEEK 7
WEEK 8
WEEK 9
WEEK 10

REGULAR

25.

efface
v.

to wipe out; do away with

Five years of absence did nothing to efface the vivid memories of his violent temper.

26.

effectual
adj.

efficient

The medication I took yesterday appears to be effectual; I'm feeling better by the hour.

27.

effeminate
adj.

having womanish traits or qualities

Jay's parents worry that his effeminate way of speaking will get him in trouble with the football team.

28.

effervescent
adj.

enthusiastic; bubbling

The cheerleaders were even effervescent in class, organizing cheers for their teachers.

29.

effusion
n.

an outpouring

The effusion of public support during the royal family's time of crisis warmed the Queen's heart.

30.

egotistical
adj.

pertaining to or characterized by a sense of excessive pride and self-importance

He thinks he is a take-charge kind of person, but he's really an egotistical control freak.

31.

elation
n.

a feeling or state of great joy or pride; exultant gladness; high spirits

The feeling of sheer elation upon winning the Tour de France made all the years of training worth it.

32.

elegiac
adj.

mournful, expressing sorrow, usually through poetic form

The elegiac poem read at the funeral of Mr. Pauly left us all with a sad, melancholy spirit.

33.
elicit
v.

to bring about a response; to draw out information; to call forth emotion

The touching speech was designed to elicit grief from all who heard it.

34.
elite
n.

the choice or best of anything considered collectively, as of a group or class of persons

An elite gathering of the most gifted physicists promises to yield startling discoveries about the origin of the universe.

35.
elucidate
v.

to bring out more clearly the facts concerning (something)

Martin was unable to offer an explanation that might elucidate his strange behavior.

36.
elude
v.

to evade the search or pursuit of by dexterity or artifice

Wild Bill managed to elude capture for many years but was finally shot and killed in Nevada.

37.
embed
v.

to place firmly into a surrounding mass

After searing through the atmosphere, the meteorite embedded in the soft sandstone face of the hill.

38.
embezzle
v.

to take fraudulently for one's own use, as money or property entrusted to one's care

Jack was sentenced to fifteen years because he had embezzled $600,000 from the company funds.

39.
embroil
v.

to become involved

"Try not to become embroiled in your sister's little dramas," my mother advised.

40.
embryonic
adj.

related to the beginning stages

Our program is just beginning; it is in its embryonic stage.

WEEK 1
WEEK 2
WEEK 3
WEEK 4
WEEK 5
WEEK 6
WEEK 7
WEEK 8
WEEK 9
WEEK 10

REGULAR

41.

emigrate
v.

to go from one country, state, or region for the purpose of settling or residing in another

Scientists believe that the earliest Indians emigrated from Asia and arrived in North America thousands of years ago.

42.

eminence
n.

an elevated position with respect to rank, place, character, condition, etc.

Sandra Bullock was recognized as an actress of great eminence after she recieved an Oscar.

43.

emit
v.

to send or give out

The strange looking device emitted an unusual beeping sound, but we couldn't figure out what it was.

44.

enchant
v.

to subject to magical influence; bewitch

Jasper was enchanted by the hypnotist's swaying silver charm.

45.

encumber
v.

to impede with obstacles

Walking up the stairs encumbered by two laundry baskets and a towel over my head, I naturally tripped and broke my ankle.

46.

endow
v.

to provide with a permanent fund or source of income

The wealthy millionaire endowed the school with a huge gift for the building of a new auditorium.

47.

enfranchise
v.

to endow with a privilege, especially with the right to vote

Women were not enfranchised until as late as the 1920s with the passage of the Nineteenth Amendment.

48.

engaging
adj.

charming; attractive

While your story is very engaging at the outset, it becomes dull towards the end.

49.

engender
v.

to produce, cause, or give rise to

Small crimes, such as vandalism, may engender greater crimes if not quickly suppressed.

50.

engross
v.

to occupy completely

The vivid story line and interesting cast of characters completely engrossed me, so I didn't realize that five hours had gone by.

51.

enigma
n.

a puzzling or inexplicable occurrence or situation

The new traffic pattern seemed an enigma to the community that had grown used to the straighter, more direct route.

52.

enmity
n.

a feeling or condition of hostility; hatred; ill will; animosity; antagonism

Their mutual enmity was evident even to unsuspecting bystanders.

53.

ennoble
v.

to give dignity or honor to

Though he pursued his charity work in a humble manner, helping others served to ennoble him and fill him with a sense of righteousness.

54.

enrapture
v.

to delight extravagantly or intensely

The audience was enraptured with the hero's triumph.

55.

enshrine
v.

to keep sacred

The saint's tomb was enshrined in a beautiful temple erected to commemorate her extraordinary life.

56.

ensue
v.

to follow in order; come afterward, esp. in immediate succession

Chaos ensued when smoke filled the cafeteria in the school during lunch.

WEEK 1
WEEK 2
WEEK 3
WEEK 4
WEEK 5
WEEK 6
WEEK 7
WEEK 8
WEEK 9
WEEK 10

REGULAR

57.

entail   v.

to involve; necessitate

Your job responsibilities entail typing, taking phone calls, and bringing coffee to the boss.

58.

enthrall   v.

to captivate, or charm

"CATS" was a very popular Broadway show that entralled thousands of viewers.

59.

entice   v.

to lead on by exciting hope or desire; allure

A nice piece of rich German chocolate cake can entice even the most disciplined of dieters.

60.

entwine   v.

to tie or twist together; to link together

Now that their futures were entwined, the newly married couple set forth to begin their life together.

61.

enunciate   v.

to utter or pronounce (words, sentences, etc.), esp. in an articulate or a particular manner

The interpreters were taught to enunciate clearly to avoid any language-related confusion.

62.

epidemic   n.

wide-spread occurrence of a disease in a certain region

The disease was mistakenly referred to as an epidemic when in fact only a few cases had been reported.

63.

epitome   n.

a person or thing that is typical of or possesses to a high degree the features of a whole class

The epitome of grace and sophistication, Grace Kelly looked like she had stepped out of a portrait.

64.

epoch   n.

a particular period of time marked by distinctive features, events, etc.

In Roman history, the epoch of Julius Caesar was one of the most fascinating times the world has known.

65.

equilibrium   n.

a state of balance

When two chemicals are in a state of equilibrium, the rate of chemicals entering and exiting is identical.

66.

equitable   adj.

characterized by fairness

Jacob did not feel that there had been an equitable distribution of cookies among him and his brothers.

67.

equivocate   v.

to use unclear and somewhat deceptive expressions in order to avoid commitment

When asked about his position on disarmament, the candidate only equivocated.

68.

eradicate   v.

to remove or destroy utterly

Scientists had hoped that penicillin would eradicate many afflictions that would cripple or even kill many people.

69.

erratic   adj.

notably inconsistent; deviating from the usual or proper course in conduct or opinion

His driving was erratic; sometimes he sped as though he would be late, then would suddenly slow to a crawl.

70.

erudite   adj.

characterized by great knowledge; learned or scholarly

The erudite professor can handle any literary reference you can throw his way; he'll know what you're talking about.

71.

escalate   v.

to increase in intensity, magnitude

Their bickering soon escalated into a major fight between the two brothers.

72.

esteem   n.

favorable opinion or judgment; (v.) to regard highly or favorably; to consider as of a certain value or of a certain type

She held her boss in high esteem because of the friendly, though professional, manner in which he addressed his staff.

WEEK 1
WEEK 2
WEEK 3
WEEK 4
WEEK 5
WEEK 6
WEEK 7
WEEK 8
WEEK 9
WEEK 10

REGULAR

73.

estrange
v.

to make hostile, unsympathetic, or indifferent; alienate

Emily and her mother were still estranged from each other ten years after they had fought.

74.

etiquette
n.

conventional requirements as to social behavior; proprieties of conduct as established in any class or community or for any occasion

Donna was well known for holding high standards of etiquette, making sure that all proper social rules were followed.

75.

eulogy
n.

a speech or writing in praise of a person or thing, esp. a set oration in honor of a deceased person

Several businessmen gave lofty eulogies at the funeral of the CEO of the major corporation.

76.

euphemism
n.

the substitution of a mild, indirect, or vague expression for one thought to be offensive, harsh, or blunt

When some hospitals state that an elderly person "expired," it is simply a euphemism for the fact that he or she died.

77.

evoke
v.

to call or summon forth, usually emotions or memories

His poetry evokes the feelings of solitude and serenity often felt in nature.

78.

exacerbate
v.

to increase the severity, bitterness, or violence of (disease, ill feeling, etc.); aggravate

Her dismal outlook was only exacerbated by the death of her beloved goldfish.

79.

excruciating
adj.

extremely painful; causing intense suffering; unbearably distressing; torturing

The soldier was in excruciating pain after the army surgeons were forced to amputate his leg without anesthesia.

80.

exemplary
adj.

worthy of imitation; commendable

Your A+ shows exemplary work in understanding electromagnetism.

81.

exemplify   v.

to show by example

The fashion designer's line exemplifies the minimalist spirit; the label has clean lines and simple, classic shapes.

82.

exhaustive   adj.

thorough and complete in execution

Because language changes so rapidly, no dictionary can be an exhaustive listing of every word in the lexicon.

83.

exhort   v.

to urge, advise, or caution earnestly; admonish urgently

The preacher exhorted the congregation to boycott the new movie, claiming that it promoted witchcraft.

84.

exigent   adj.

urgent

Under exigent circumstances, such as a fire, chances are you won't have time to collect your belongings.

85.

exile   v.

to expel or banish (a person) from his or her country; expatriate; (n.) expulsion from one's native land by authoritative decree

Henry of West Anglia was exiled for his involvement in the plot to overthrow the Duke of Earl.

86.

exotic   adj.

from another part of the world; foreign; intriguingly different

For her honeymoon, Daphne wanted to travel to some remote, exotic island in the Pacific.

87.

expatriate   v.

to banish (a person) from his or her native country; (adj.) exiled

Because of his controversial novel, Salman Rushdie was expatriated from India, and forced to relocate to England.

88.

expediency   n.

the use of methods that are advantageous rather than fair or just; the quality of being appropriate for a purpose, especially when that purpose is self-serving

The selfish politician was more guided by expediency than by moral principle.

WEEK 1
WEEK 2
WEEK 3
WEEK 4
WEEK 5
WEEK 6
WEEK 7
WEEK 8
WEEK 9
WEEK 10

REGULAR

89.

expend
v.

to spend; use up

Since I had expended so much energy on this project, I was in tears when I discovered that we didn't win the prize.

90.

expertise
n.

expert skill or knowledge; expertness; know-how

I need your expertise in order to make this plant operate more efficiently.

91.

explicate
v.

to make clear the meaning of; to explain

Our instructor explicated the grammatical concepts until each and every student could demonstrate understanding.

92.

expulsion
n.

forcible ejection

The pilot's expulsion from the cockpit was completely unintended; he had accidentally hit the Eject button.

93.

expunge
v.

to strike or blot out; erase

The lawyer wanted nothing more than to expunge the offending statements from the court record.

94.

exquisite
adj.

of special beauty or charm; of rare and appealing excellence

My wedding dress was an exquisite Chinese costume made of silk and embroidery.

95.

exterminate
v.

to get rid of by destroying; destroy totally

Pete's Pest Services will exterminate all ants and cockroaches in your house within two hours or your money back.

96.

extol
v.

to praise in the highest terms

While we often extol the virtue of honesty, each of us is no stranger to deceit.

WEEK
1

WEEK
2

WEEK
3

WEEK
4

WEEK
5

WEEK
6

WEEK
7

WEEK
8

WEEK
9

WEEK
10

REGULAR

97.

extort   v.

to obtain by violence, threats, compulsion, or the subjection of another to some necessity

The criminals tried to extort money from the wealthy painter by threatening to reveal his deepest secrets.

98.

extradite   v.

to give a fugitive over to the jurisdiction of another country

TThe Cuban government decided to extradite the criminal who fled to Cuba after committing three murders in the U.S.

99.

extraneous   adj.

having no essential relation to a subject

The editor whittled away all the extraneous details until he was left with only the main story line.

100.

extravagance   n.

excessive spending of money

The hotel heiress was known for her extravagance, although she could certainly afford being wasteful because she had so much money.

A. Fill in the appropriate words using the clues below.

across:

1) adj. overflowing with fervor, enthusiasm, or excitement; high spirited
4) v. to bring out more clearly the facts concerning (something)
5) adj. having no essential relation to a subject
6) v. to strip, specifically of ceremonial clothes, ornaments, or military equipment
7) adj. urgent

down:

2) n. the use of methods that are advantageous rather than fair or just; the quality of being appropriate for a purpose, especially when that purpose is self-serving
3) adj. bewildered
4) v. to build up, or strengthen, especially in moral or religion
5) v. to follow in order; come afterward, esp. in immediate succession
8) v. to send or give out

B. Match the words on the left with their appropriate definitions on the right.

A. disseminate _____ 1. adj. easy to manage

B. dissipate _____ 2. adj. enthusiastic; bubbling

C. docile _____ 3. n. a speech or writing in praise of a person or thing, esp. in honor of a deceased person

D. dogmatic _____ 4. v. to scatter or spread widely, as though sowing seed; promulgate extensively; broadcast; disperse

E. earnest _____ 5. v. to involve; necessitate

F. eccentric _____ 6. v. to praise in the highest terms

G. ecstatic _____ 7. v. to disperse or disappear

H. effervescent _____ 8. adj. joyful

I. elegiac _____ 9. adj. mournful, expressing sorrow, usually through poetic form

J. encumber _____ 10. adj. having or showing deep sincerity or seriousness

K. enigma _____ 11. adj. deviating from the recognized or customary character, practice, etc.

L. entail _____ 12. n. a person or thing that is typical of or possesses to a high degree the features of a whole class

M. epitome _____ 13. v. to increase the severity, bitterness, or violence of (disease, ill feeling, etc.); aggravate

N. equilibrium _____ 14. v. to strike or blot out; erase

O. erudite _____ 15. v. to urge, advise, or caution earnestly; admonish urgently

P. eulogy _____ 16. adj. characterized by great knowledge; learned or scholarly

Q. exacerbate _____ 17. n. a state of balance

R. exhort _____ 18. n. a puzzling or inexplicable occurrence or situation

S. expunge _____ 19. adj. making statements, often arrogantly, without argument or evidence

T. extol _____ 20. v. to impede with obstacles

300pts

100pts

Week 5

flux

forerun

noun

"The difference between the impossible and the possible lies in a person's determination."
- Tommy Lasorda

verb

Start   Restart

1.

exult
v.

to rejoice or feel happy

The entire village exulted when one of their own killed the enemy with a stone and slingshot; the villagers were finally rid of the menacing giant.

2.

fabricate
v.

to make or build; to invent a story or a lie

Danny fabricated his tale to confuse his parents about where he had been the night before.

3.

façade
n.

a superficial appearance; the false front of a building

The façade of the building was painted to look like a New York brownstone when it was actually made of flat concrete.

4.

facetious
adj.

not meant to be taken seriously or literally

We all knew that Emily was being facetious when she said that her skinny 13-year-old brother was a muscular hunk.

5.

facile
adj.

moving, acting, working, proceeding, etc., with ease, sometimes with superficiality

Knowing a more facile method of performing the same action will save a lot of time and manpower.

6.

fanatic
n.

a religious zealot

The fanatic set fire to the building, claiming that he had a divine mission to bring about the day of judgment.

7.

fatuous
adj.

idiotic

The nutty professor has been making fatuous claims about little green men from Mars.

8.

felony
n.

one of the highest class of offenses, and punishable with death or imprisonment

Vehicular manslaughter is a felony, while a traffic violation is a misdemeanor.

9.

ferocious   adj.

of a wild, fierce, and savage nature

There were rumors of a ferocious tiger that lived on the mountain and ate everyone who came near it.

10.

fervor   n.

passion or intensity of feeling

The minister's religious fervor shone through during his impassioned sermon.

11.

festal   adj.

joyous

The festal spirit continued from the night after the exam into the next morning, when the students were still partying.

12.

fetter   n.

chains or handcuffs

The fetters around the feet of the prisoner prevented him from making a successful escape because they hindered his movements.

13.

finesse   n.

refinement and delicacy of performance, execution, or artisanship

Let's try to handle this problem with a little more calm and finesse.

14.

fiscal   adj.

pertaining to the treasury or public finances

This fiscal quarter has brought a 5% increase in earnings for our corporation.

15.

fitful   adj.

spasmodic, restless

A fitful sleep full of strange dreams plagued the lonely camper on her first night in the woods.

16.

flagrant   adj.

noticeably bad or offensive

We were all enraged when the referee didn't call the player on his flagrant foul.

WEEK 1
WEEK 2
WEEK 3
WEEK 4
WEEK 5
WEEK 6
WEEK 7
WEEK 8
WEEK 9
WEEK 10

REGULAR

17. flamboyant adj.

characterized by extravagance and in general by lack of good taste

In spite of her flamboyant dress, Jane made an excellent impression during her job interview.

18. flaunt v.

to show off

Although Greg lived well off his trust fund money, he never flaunted his wealth.

19. fledgling n.

a young bird; a young or inexperienced person

The fledgling reporter didn't know any of the tricks of the trade and waited patiently outside while the other reporters elbowed their way into the pressroom.

20. flora n.

the plants of a particular region

The exotic jungle flora included bright pink flowers and lush, purple fruits.

21. florid adj.

flushed with red; very ornate; flowery

The florid speech was obviously filled with exaggerations and overly colorful language.

22. fluctuate v.

to change continually; shift back and forth; vary irregularly

The weather today has fluctuated from hot and dry to cold and wet since early this afternoon.

23. flux n.

a state of constant movement, change, or renewal

The state's budget is in a constant state of flux because many factors, including federal funding and overseas markets, can easily change the market.

24. fodder n.

coarse food for animals

Louise saved her kitchen scraps, using them as fodder for her worms.

25.

foolhardy

adj.

recklessly or thoughtlessly bold; foolishly rash or venturesome

Four foolhardy boys attempted to scale the cliff in one afternoon and had to be rescued by the park service.

26.

forebode

v.

to be an omen or warning sign of, especially of evil

The dark, depressing clouds seemed to forebode the gloom of the coming hours.

27.

foreclose

v.

to take possession of a property bought with borrowed money because payments have not been made

Having been jobless for months, Uriah feared that he would soon be unable to pay his mortgage and that the bank would foreclose on his house.

28.

foreordain

v.

to predetermine

It seemed as though it had been foreordained that the poor, young man would rise to become king of the land.

29.

forerunner

n.

one who precedes in time; an ancestor or predecessor

The mild shaking was just a forerunner of the devastating earthquake that struck the heavily inhabited island.

30.

foreshadow

v.

to indicate or show beforehand

The early signs in the book foreshadowed the terrible unfolding of events in the later chapters.

31.

foresight

n.

perception of the nature or significance of events before they proceed

She showed remarkable foresight when she sold all her stocks the day before the major crash.

32.

forgo

v.

to deny oneself

I have decided to forgo the main course and just have cake and ice cream.

WEEK 1
WEEK 2
WEEK 3
WEEK 4
WEEK 5
WEEK 6
WEEK 7
WEEK 8
WEEK 9
WEEK 10

REGULAR

33.

formulate   v.

to express in precise form; state definitely or systematically

Kenny formulated a response that pleased his interviewers, thus granting him admission to Harvard.

34.

forthright   adj.

with directness; honest or upfront

Jake's parents appreciated his forthright answers to their questions about his whereabouts the previous night.

35.

fortitude   n.

the strenth of mind that enables one to have patience and courage despite difficulties

The soldiers showed fortitude in the face of great danger, even when they knew that very few would go home.

36.

forum   n.

an assembly or meeting place

The philosophers convened at the forum to discuss important ethical dilemmas.

37.

frank   adj.

direct and unreserved in speech; straightforward; sincere

I must be frank and not hold back my thoughts about how I feel about your mocking that poor young girl.

38.

fraternal   adj.

brotherly

The two boys have had a close, fraternal relationship since they were young.

39.

frolicsome   adj.

playful

The frolicsome students enjoyed the first day of summer vacation by playing games out in the sun, away from their books and studies.

40.

frugal   adj.

economical in use or expenditure; prudently saving or sparing; not wasteful

She was frugal, saving several bucks a week, until after a few years, she could buy her own car.

41.

fruition
n.

fulfillment; the coming into realization of a dream

The most important goal I set this year came to fruition: I was admitted to the school of my dreams.

42.

fumigate
v.

to subject to the action of smoke or fumes, especially for disinfection

We had to fumigate the house when we discovered that termites had been breeding in the attic.

43.

furtive
adj.

stealthy or sly, like the actions of a thief

The girl stole furtive glances at the handsome freshman sitting in the second row.

44.

fuse
v.

to mix together as if by melting; blend

The engineer, through fusing two different compounds, created a stronger bond to hold the steel girders in place.

45.

futile
adj.

of no use or effect; pointless

To attempt to convince your mother to allow you to get a motorcycle would be futile.

46.

gall
n.

outrageously bold rudeness

Agnes had the gall to call up her best friend at 2 in the morning when she knew that Kerry had to be at work at 5 a.m.

47.

gallant
adj.

brave, spirited, noble-minded, or chivalrous

The gallant knight rescued the beautiful princess from the evil dragon.

48.

gargantuan
adj.

gigantic; enormous; colossal

St. Peter's Basilica is a gargantuan church centered in the middle of Rome.

WEEK 1
WEEK 2
WEEK 3
WEEK 4
WEEK 5
WEEK 6
WEEK 7
WEEK 8
WEEK 9
WEEK 10
REGULAR

49.

garrison n.

a military post, especially one that is permanently established

Fort Wadsworth is a Coast Guard garrison on Staten Island.

50.

garrulous adj.

excessively talkative in a rambling, roundabout manner, esp. about trivial matters

Nicole was so garrulous that no one at the party could get a word into the conversation.

51.

gaunt adj.

extremely thin

The gaunt old man looked even thinner than he actually was because he was very tall.

52.

gawky adj.

awkward; clumsy

Sam turned into a gawky teenager, well over six feet in height, but no more than 125 pounds in weight.

53.

genesis n.

creation

The inventor was often asked to describe the genesis of his amazing idea.

54.

genial adj.

cheerful, or cordial

In spite of her extremely stressful life, Laurie maintained a genial disposition.

55.

ghastly adj.

hideous

When we rescued her from the bottom of the pool, we saw that Marcy's skin had turned a ghastly shade of blue.

56.

gist n.

essence or central idea

I didn't completely understand Romeo and Juliet, but I got the gist of it after reading the Cliff Notes.

57.

glut v.

to feed or fill to satiety; sate; (n.) an excessive supply or amount; surfeit

Car dealers do not like to have a glut of used cars sitting in their lot for longer than a month.

58.

gluttonous adj.

tending to eat and drink excessively

Roman parties often were nothing more than wild feasts filled with gluttonous old men.

59.

grandeur n.

the quality of being grand or admirably great

The castle's grandeur awed the simple country folk who lived in the surrounding valleys.

60.

grandiloquence n.

speech that is overblown, often to the point of being pompous or bombastic

Everyone rolled their eyes since the speech by the political candidate was noted for its grandiloquence.

61.

grandiose adj.

having an imposing style or effect; longer than needed

The keynote speaker's grandiose style was full of flowery language and dramatic expression, but short on actual content.

62.

granulate v.

to form into grains or small particles

The salt granulates easily when dried and crushed into a fine powder.

63.

gratify v.

to please, as by satisfying a physical or mental desire or need

I gratified my appetite by eating a five-course meal.

64.

gravity n.

seriousness

The surgeon explained the gravity of the situation to the waiting family members.

WEEK 1
WEEK 2
WEEK 3
WEEK 4
WEEK 5
WEEK 6
WEEK 7
WEEK 8
WEEK 9
WEEK 10
REGULAR

65.

graze

v.

to feed on growing grass and herbage

Living in the countryside, we usually see cows graze lazily on the hills just beyond our home.

66.

grisly

adj.

fear-inspiring

The grisly murder scene frightened even the detectives on the case who thought they had already seen it all.

67.

grovel

v.

to humble oneself or act in an abject manner, as in great fear or utter servility

The beggars groveled at the feet of the wealthy in hopes of picking up a few coins.

68.

guile

n.

treacherous cunning; skillful deceit

We knew of her guile only later, when we discovered that Captain Fox had been a double agent all along.

69.

guileless

adj.

honest; without deception

Becky's smile and guileless ways helped her win the election.

70.

gutless

adj.

lacking courage, fortitude, or determination

The gutless coward could not face his duties so he ran away.

71.

hackneyed

adj.

to make stale or dull by repetition

The hackneyed expression was so overused that the politician immediately lost credibility for repeating it.

72.

hale

adj.

of sound and vigorous health

The teenager, hale and hearty again after the flu, was back to his old form and eating everything in sight.

73.
haphazard
adj.

dependent on mere chance

Don't expect to win the game if you only practice haphazardly!

74.
hardihood
n.

foolish, daring

The teenager's hardihood was in full evidence when she climbed up into the theater's catwalk.

75.
haughty
adj.

scornfully and condescendingly proud

With a haughty toss of her head, the queen rejected the humble fare presented her and left the room.

76.
hazardous
adj.

full of risk; perilous; risky

The cones on the highway helped to guide the cars around the hazardous construction still going on down the road.

77.
heathen
n.

an irreligious or uncivilized person

Pauline hesitated to invite Bob to the wedding, for he always acted like a heathen when he drank.

78.
heckle
v.

to try to irritate or annoy (someone speaking or performing in public) with questions

The two men in the back heckled the speaker until he left the stage in embarrassment.

79.
heedless
adj.

thoughtless

The heedless child was accustomed to getting her own way and never cared about pleasing others.

80.
heinous
adj.

extremely wicked; evil

The heinous crimes appeared on the front page of the newspapers the next day, making the readers shudder at the horror of the actions of the criminals.

WEEK 1
WEEK 2
WEEK 3
WEEK 4
WEEK 5
WEEK 6
WEEK 7
WEEK 8
WEEK 9
WEEK 10

REGULAR

81.
hereditary   adj.

passing, or capable of passing, naturally from parent to offspring through the genes

The Smiths unfortunately had a hereditary gene that caused all the women in the family to develop breast cancer.

82.
heresy   n.

an opinion or doctrine subversive of settled beliefs or accepted principles

The King denounced Paine's pamphlet as a heresy and demanded that he be thrown in jail for publishing such a subversive work.

83.
hermit   n.

a person who has withdrawn from society and lives a solitary existence; a recluse

The hermit has been sighted just once in the twenty years he has lived here; he clearly prefers to remain locked up in his little hut.

84.
heterogeneous   adj.

consisting of dissimilar elements or ingredients of different kinds

While never having been monolithic, the population of the United States has become increasingly heterogeneous in recent decades.

85.
hiatus   n.

break, gap, interim

After a brief hiatus on a high branch, the hummingbird commenced foraging for nectar among the flowers of the garden.

86.
hoard   v.

to gather and store away for the sake of accumulation

The greedy, chubby child hoarded all the candy from the piñata and wouldn't share with his classmates.

87.
homely   adj.

not attractive or good-looking

The woman was homely in appearance, but her million dollar inheritance improved her looks considerably.

88.
homogeneous   adj.

made up of similar parts or elements

The population of our town was once rather homogenous, but now people from all over the world live here.

89.

hoodwink

v.

to deceive or trick

The internet scam hoodwinked unsuspecting folks who believed that they could get the new iPod for free.

90.

horde

n.

a gathered multitude of human beings

The horde tried to shove their way into the store for the huge Black Friday sales.

91.

hustle

v.

to move with haste and promptness

We had to hustle through the station to catch the train on time.

92.

hypocrisy

n.

extreme insincerity

Some suggest that for the U.S. to keep nuclear weapons while ordering others to destroy them is sheer hypocrisy.

93.

hypothesis

n.

a proposition taken for granted as a premise from which to reach a conclusion

A scientific hypothesis that survives experimental testing becomes a scientific theory.

94.

illegitimate

adj.

unlawfully brought into existence

Sarah divorced her husband of twenty years when she discovered that he had fathered three illegitimate children.

95.

illiberal

adj.

stingy

An illiberal disposition in a child is most disheartening to its parents.

96.

illicit

adj.

unlawful

The last war between the two countries erupted over accusations that both had engaged in illicit trade with its neighbors.

WEEK 1
WEEK 2
WEEK 3
WEEK 4
WEEK 5
WEEK 6
WEEK 7
WEEK 8
WEEK 9
WEEK 10

REGULAR

97.
illusion   n.

something that deceives by producing a false or misleading impression of reality

A mirage in the desert is simply an illusion that the heat and the sun play on your mind.

98.
illustrious   adj.

well known and very distinguished; eminent

The illustrious composer wrote one final piece to cap off his spectacularly successful career.

99.
immaculate   adj.

without spot or blemish

We wiped down the kitchen until it was immaculate and every surface was gleaming white.

100.
imminence   n.

the quality or condition of being about to occur; something about to occur

The imminence of danger was foreshadowed by the sound of thunder and the eerie howling sound outside.

A. Fill in the appropriate words using the clues below.

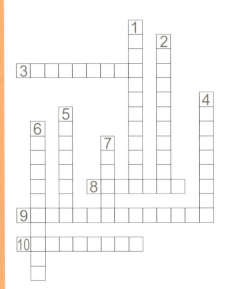

across:

3) v. to change continually; shift back and forth; vary irregularly
8) n. refinement and delicacy of performance, execution, or artisanship
9) n. speech that is overblown, often to the point of being pompous or bombastic
10) v. to take possession of a property bought with borrowed money because payments have not been made

down:

1) adj. unlawfully brought into existence
2) adj. made up of similar parts or elements
4) v. to make or build; to invent a story or a lie
5) n. fulfillment; the coming into realization of a dream
6) adj. well known and very distinguished; eminent
7) adj. cheerful, or cordial

B. Match the words on the left with their appropriate definitions on the right.

A. façade _____
B. facetious _____
C. fervor _____
D. fiscal _____
E. flagrant _____
F. foolhardy _____
G. forebode _____
H. forgo _____
I. fortitude _____
J. frugal _____
K. furtive _____
L. garrulous _____
M. gist _____
N. grandiose _____
O. guile _____
P. hackneyed _____
Q. heinous _____
R. hiatus _____
S. illicit _____
T. immaculate _____

1. adj. having an imposing style or effect; longer than needed
2. adj. to make stale or dull by repetition
3. adj. pertaining to the treasury or public finances
4. v. to be an omen or warning sign of, especially of evil
5. n. passion or intensity of feeling
6. n. treacherous cunning; skillful deceit
7. n. essence or central idea
8. adj. excessively talkative in a rambling, round-about manner, esp. about trivial matters
9. adj. extremely wicked; evil
10. adj. recklessly or thoughtlessly bold; foolishly rash or venturesome
11. n. the strenth of mind that enables one to have patience and courage despite difficulties
12. n. a superficial appearance; the false front of a builidng
13. adj. stealthy or sly, like the actions of a thief
14. adj. noticeably bad or offensive
15. adj. not meant to be taken seriously or literally
16. adj. economical in use or expenditure; prudently saving or sparing; not wasteful
17. n. break, gap, interim
18. adj. without spot or blemish
19. v. to deny oneself
20. adj. unlawful

100pts

300pts

Week 6

impel

incipient

 "You must motivate yourself everyday!"
- Matthew Stasior

verb

adj.

Start   Restart

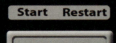

 A

 B

1.

imminent   adj.

dangerous and close at hand

Superman, sensing the baby was in imminent danger, swooped down to remove her from harm's way.

2.

immutable   adj.

unchangeable

Darwin did not view species as immutable beings, but as subject to the transformative forces of evolution.

3.

impasse   n.

a road or passage having no exit

Proceedings reached an impasse when the issue of who would pay for the caterer arose.

4.

impassioned   adj.

filled with passion; fervent

The former Vice President made an impassioned speech about the importance of protecting our environment.

5.

impede   v.

to slow in movement or progress by means of obstacles or hindrances; obstruct; hinder

The threat of another avalanche impeded the effort to rescue the skiers.

6.

impel   v.

to drive or urge forward

Seeing pictures of the refugees in the region of conflict impelled us to travel to the area to offer medical aid.

7.

impenetrable   adj.

that cannot be penetrated, pierced, entered

She got lost in what appeared to be an impenetrable forest, hidden from any possibility of escape.

8.

imperil   v.

to endanger

The leniency of airport security prior to the September 11th terrorist attacks imperiled the lives of many innocent citizens.

WEEK 1
WEEK 2
WEEK 3
WEEK 4
WEEK 5
WEEK 6
WEEK 7
WEEK 8
WEEK 9
WEEK 10

REGULAR

9.

impermeable adj.

not able to soak through; impassable

The bathroom was difficult to clean since the layer of scum seemed to be impermeable.

10.

impertinence n.

rudeness

It is common for young children to test their parents' authority with disturbing displays of impertinence.

11.

impervious adj.

not easily affected

Seal the edges of the sink with caulk to render the edges impervious to water.

12.

impetuous adj.

impulsive

The impetuous child darted out into the street and was nearly hit by a car.

13.

impiety n.

irreverence toward God

People who harbor anger against religion or religious people often act with impeity.

14.

implicate v.

to show or prove to be involved in or concerned

The first robber implicated two other people in an effort to tell the truth to the jury and to reduce his own sentence.

15.

impolitic adj.

not advisable; unwise

The TV host's impolitic treatment of a sensitive issue angered millions of Americans.

16.

impoverished adj.

poor

Dorothy designed simple housing developments for the impoverished farmers in her county.

17.

impregnable adj.

strong enough to resist or withstand attack; not to be taken by force, unconquerable

The fortress, with its three gun turrets and foot-thick walls, is impregnable.

18.

impressionable adj.

easily impressed or influenced; susceptible

Her class was quite impressionable, since half of her students went on to major in that field in college.

19.

impromptu adj.

made or done without previous preparation; (adv.) without preparation; (n.) something impromptu

In many comedy clubs, performers are required to do impromptu skits that they have had no time to rehearse.

20.

improvise v.

to compose and perform or deliver without previous preparation

He improvised the jazz piece simply from three notes.

21.

impudence n.

offensive in a bold and disrespectful manner

Bobby was punished for the impudence he had demonstrated with the sarcastic remarks to his sister.

22.

impulsive adj.

characterized by actions based on sudden desires, whims, or inclinations rather than careful thought

Brian was impulsive, suddenly getting up at work, walking over and interrupting almost anyone he chose at any time.

23.

inane adj.

silly

The cheerleaders talked of inane subjects, such as their hair, boys, and chewing gum.

24.

inanimate adj.

without the qualities associated with active, living organisms

Some people think that plants are inanimate beings, but studies indicate that they are sensitive to our emotions.

WEEK 1
WEEK 2
WEEK 3
WEEK 4
WEEK 5
WEEK 6
WEEK 7
WEEK 8
WEEK 9
WEEK 10

REGULAR

25.

inbred   adj.

naturally inherent; innate; native

That horse's speed was inbred; the horse was descended from a long line of thoroughbreds.

26.

incapacitate   v.

to deprive of power, capacity, competency, or qualification

The CEO's powers were incapacitated by the Board of Trustees after constant complaints of his abusive handling of so many problem issues in the corporation.

27.

incarcerate   v.

to imprison

The judge ordered the officers to incarcerate the serial killer before he could do any more damage to society.

28.

incinerate   v.

to reduce to ashes; to burn completely

He incinerated any documents that would indicate he went along with the plot to overthrow the government.

29.

incipient   adj.

beginning to exist or appear; in an initial stage

It takes time to get a business going from its incipient stage until the time it begins making a profit.

30.

incongruous   adj.

unsuitable for the time, place, or occasion

The bright pink plastic chair was an incongruous addition to a tawny room full of Chippendale furniture.

31.

inconspicuous   adj.

not noticeable; unable to be seen

Do not worry about the stain on the sleeve of your dress; it is inconspicuous.

32.

incontestable   adj.

not contestable; not open to dispute; incontrovertible

The answers given were incontestable; the judges would not compromise with any challenges.

33.

incontrovertible adj.

indisputable

Scientists now consider the evidence for global warming to be incontrovertible.

34.

incorporate v.

to put or introduce into a body or mass as an integral part or parts

He incorporated all her recommendations into his model for how to build the bridge.

35.

indefatigable adj.

tireless

The speakers were indefatigable and traveled the country many times over, trying to teach young people about patriotic values.

36.

indignity n.

unmerited contemptuous conduct or treatment

The indignity of undergoing a strip search at the local jail was enough to keep me out of jail for the rest of my life.

37.

indiscernible adj.

not perceptible

The headmaster's expression was indiscernible, and I couldn't tell whether he was smiling or frowning at me.

38.

indiscreet adj.

lacking wise judgment

The indiscreet CEO accidentally leaked an important company secret to the press.

39.

indiscriminate adj.

not choosy

The woman chose her fruits and vegetables in an indiscriminate manner, randomly throwing items into several bags she had brought with her to the supermarket.

40.

indisputable adj.

not disputable or deniable; incontestable

It is indisputable that America was developed to be a country valuing freedom above all else.

WEEK 1
WEEK 2
WEEK 3
WEEK 4
WEEK 5
WEEK 6
WEEK 7
WEEK 8
WEEK 9
WEEK 10

REGULAR

41.

indoctrination v.

to instruct in a body of doctrine or principles

Some educational systems are more concerned with indoctrination than with teaching students to think creatively for themselves.

42.

indomitable adj.

unconquerable

The cancer patient's indomitable spirit, in the face of overwhelming odds, inspired even the doctors.

43.

induct v.

to bring in

The record director was inducted into the Rock and Roll Hall of Fame in 1989.

44.

inept adj.

without skill or aptitude for a particular task or assignment

An inept worker will probably not last very long at this job since it requires a lot of skill.

45.

ineradicable adj.

unable to be removed, erased, or destroyed

The earliest memories from my troubled childhood are ineradicably etched into my mind.

46.

inert adj.

having no inherent power of action, motion, or resistance; not moving or not changing

Inert gases do not readily react with other elements.

47.

inexpedient adj.

inadvisable

Declaring war on two fronts across both the Atlantic and Pacific Ocean is an inexpedient tactic.

48.

infidelity n.

disloyalty

The woman discovered her husband's infidelity after twenty years of marriage, and promptly divorced him.

49.

influx
n.

infusion; flow in of a large number

The influx of Chinese immigrants during the building of the transcontinental railroad in the nineteenth century led to racism and prejudice.

50.

ingenious
adj.

characterized by cleverness or originality of invention or construction

Your invention of a potato chip bag that doubles as a temporary TV remote control is simply ingenious.

51.

ingratiate
v.

to establish (oneself) in the favor or good graces of others, esp. by deliberate effort (usually fol. by with)

Nathan ingratiated himself with his teacher in order to get a better grade on his final.

52.

inherent
adj.

intrinsic

The mistakes in the math problem were inherent in the question; the numbers given were already flawed.

53.

inhibit
v.

to hold back or in

Normally rather inhibited around strangers, Marcie introduced herself to three new people at the party.

54.

innate
adj.

existing in one from birth; inborn; native

Her shy nature seemed innate; she had shied away from most people even as an infant.

55.

innocuous
adj.

harmless

Vaccines, although strains of bacteria, are innocuous to most humans.

56.

inoculate
v.

to give a booster shot

The nurse inoculated the child with a polio vaccine.

WEEK 1
WEEK 2
WEEK 3
WEEK 4
WEEK 5
WEEK 6
WEEK 7
WEEK 8
WEEK 9
WEEK 10

REGULAR

57.

inquisition
n.

a court or tribunal for examination
and punishment of heretics

The church established the Inquisition
to root out suspected heretics.

58.

insatiable
adj.

impossible to satisfy

The best students usually have an
insatiable appetite for learning,
soaking up everything they read and
hear.

59.

insidious
adj.

intended to entrap or beguile,
treacherous

An interrogator may use insidious
methods of getting information about
his enemy's weaknesses.

60.

insipid
adj.

lacking flavor or zest; dull

Angie finally grew weary of her little
sister's insipid personality.

61.

insolent
adj.

bold rudeness; casual and arrogant
disprespect

Tom Drakeson is an insolent little boy,
disrespectful to all of his elders.

62.

instigate
v.

to provoke

The bully likes to instigate playground
fights by taunting others and picking
on those smaller than he is.

63.

insufferable
adj.

intolerable

The prisoners endured insufferable
conditions for years before their
rescue.

64.

insuperable
adj.

impossible to overcome

We were ten against one hundred
and faced what appeared to be
insuperable odds.

65.

insurgence n.

uprising

The peasant insurgence in the Middle Kingdom aimed to overthrow the corrupt government and install a democratic leader.

66.

insurrection n.

the state of being in active resistance to authority

The insurrection worried the general, who knew that if the people massed together they might overwhelm the army.

67.

interim n.

time between acts or periods

You should wait six to eight weeks for a decision; in the interim, feel free to call our office.

68.

intermingle v.

to mingle, one with another; intermix

The crowds would intermingle every Sunday in the park, taking advantage of the wonderful weather Spring brought to the community.

69.

interpose v.

to come between other things or persons

She often interposed herself whenever there was a problem in the family, even though the family dreaded her involvement.

70.

intervene v.

to interfere for some reason

After the bar-room brawl broke out, several bystanders intervened to pull the men apart.

71.

intractable adj.

not easily controlled or directed; not docile or manageable; stubborn; obstinate

The intractable horse wouldn't stop throwing his rider and thrashing around in the barn.

72.

intransigent adj.

uncompromising; stubborn

Igor was an intransigent fellow; he never wavered from his belief that the world is flat.

WEEK 1
WEEK 2
WEEK 3
WEEK 4
WEEK 5
WEEK 6
WEEK 7
WEEK 8
WEEK 9
WEEK 10

REGULAR

73.

intrepid   adj.

resolutely fearless

The military looks for brave men and women, intrepid souls who will bravely march into battle.

74.

intrinsic   adj.

belonging to a thing by its very nature

The SAT has an intrinsic difficulty, and students must refine their logic and comprehension skills to overcome it.

75.

inundation   n.

flood

The inundation of phone calls following the episode of American Idol resulted in our hiring ten new telephone operators.

76.

invariable   adj.

unchangeable

Because of the massive problems with insects, prohibiting drinks and foods in classrooms is an invariable rule.

77.

irascible   adj.

easily provoked to anger; very irritable

Scrooge is an irascible old man who eventually learns the power of love.

78.

irk   v.

to afflict with pain, irritation, or fatigue

The students' babble began to irk Mrs. Cheng, so she made them put their heads down on their desks.

79.

irradiance   n.

luster

The irradiance of the diamond was amazing to behold.

80.

irreducible   adj.

impossible to reduce to a desired, simpler, or smaller form or amount

Scientists believed that the atom was an irreducible form until they discovered electrons, protons, and neutrons.

81.

jocose adj.

given to or characterized by joking; jesting; humorous; playful

His jocose nature made him the life of the party.

82.

jocular adj.

given to, characterized by, intended for, or suited to joking or jesting

The jocular young man tended to make fun of everything.

83.

jovial adj.

merry

Santa Claus was jovial, laughing heartily and letting all the little kids tug on his big white beard.

84.

judicious adj.

prudent; cautious

The young man, despite his age, was judicious and careful in considering all aspects of his problems.

85.

jurisdiction n.

lawful power or right to exercise official authority

The police officer stopped me for speeding but could not give me a ticket because he was out of his jurisdiction.

86.

lacerate v.

to tear rudely or raggedly; cut deeply

Joe accidentally lacerated his arm when he slipped on the floor while he was cutting meat to prepare for his dinner.

87.

laconic adj.

terse, concise, using few words

Long hours of meditation had made Keiko quite laconic.

88.

lampoon n.

sharp, often virulent satire ridiculing severely the character or behavior of a person, society, etc.; (v.) to mock or ridicule in a lampoon

Saturday Night Live is often an effective lampoon of our politics and society.

WEEK 1
WEEK 2
WEEK 3
WEEK 4
WEEK 5
WEEK 6
WEEK 7
WEEK 8
WEEK 9
WEEK 10

REGULAR

89.
languid   adj.

fatigued

Frederick knew that he was coming down with a cold when he woke up one morning and dragged himself around the house in a languid mood.

90.
languor   n.

lack of energy or vitality; sluggishness

The languor that came from the hot day affected the mood of all those who sat in the sun.

91.
larceny   n.

theft

The thief was caught trying to steal a Ferrari from someone's driveway and was charged with larceny.

92.
laud   v.

to praise; extol

The Marine was lauded by his unit for going back into the line of fire to save his countrymen.

93.
lavish   adj.

expended or occurring in abundance; great amounts

The dining room had lavish decorations that must have cost thousands of dollars.

94.
lax   adj.

lenient; not strict

The stepfather was too lax with his new son and never tried to enforce any rules at home.

95.
leaven   v.

to make light by fermentation, as dough; to make a gradual change, especially with some moderating or enlivening influence

Tiny organisms in yeast leaven bread dough, making it rise.

96.
lethargy   n.

the quality or state of being drowsy and dull, listless and unenergetic, or indifferent and lazy; apathetic or sluggish inactivity

Kevin, late at night, gave up on his studies since he had hit such a state of lethargy that he couldn't keep his eyes open.

97.

libel   n.

defamation by written or printed
words, pictures, or in any form other
than by spoken words or gestures

The Washington Post dismissed the
libel accusations since it had
published well-supported information
that the public needed to know.

98.

limber   adj.

characterized by ease in bending the
body; supple; (v.) to make oneself
limber

Janice limbered her muscles before
she began her daily five-mile jog.

99.

limpid   adj.

clear, transparent, or pellucid, as
water, crystal, or air

Crystal Lake was called such because
it was noted for its limpid appearance.

100.

listless   adj.

having or showing little or no interest
in anything; languid; spiritless;
indifferent

They were bored and becoming
listless, hoping that he would stop
droning on and on with his speech.

A. Fill in the appropriate words using the clues below.

across:

1) adj. terse, concise, using few words
4) n. flood
6) adj. beginning to exist or appear; in an initial stage
7) adj. lenient; not strict
8) v. to slow in movement or progress by means of obstacles or hindrances; obstruct; hinder

down:

2) adj. easily provoked to anger; very irritable
3) adj. clear, transparent, or pellucid, as water, crystal, or air
4) n. infusion; flow in of a large number
5) v. to give a booster shot
8) adj. unchangeable

WEEK 1
WEEK 2
WEEK 3
WEEK 4
WEEK 5
WEEK 6
WEEK 7
WEEK 8
WEEK 9
WEEK 10

B. Match the words on the left with their appropriate definitions on the right.

A. imminent _____ 1. adj. harmless

B. impetuous _____ 2. v. to hold back or in

C. implicate _____ 3. n. offensive in a bold and disrespectful manner

D. impromptu _____ 4. v. to provoke

E. impudence _____ 5. adj. made or done without previous preparation

F. inane _____ 6. adj. resolutely fearless

G. incongruous _____ 7. adj. having no inherent power of action, motion, or resistance; not moving or not changing

H. indefatigable _____ 8. adj. silly

I. inert _____ 9. adj. fatigued

J. inhibit _____ 10. adj. given to, characterized by, intended for, or suited to joking or jesting

K. innocuous _____ 11. adj. dangerous and close at hand

L. insatiable _____ 12. adj. unsuitable for the time, place, or occasion

M. instigate _____ 13. adj. impulsive

N. intransigent _____ 14. adj. tireless

O. intrepid _____ 15. adj. uncompromising; stubborn

P. intrinsic _____ 16. adj. impossible to satisfy

Q. jocular _____ 17. adj. clear, transparent, or pellucid, as water, crystal, or air

R. languid _____ 18. adj. belonging to a thing by its very nature

S. leaven _____ 19. v. to make light by fermentation, as dough

T. limpid _____ 20. v. to show or prove to be involved in or concerned

100pts

300pts

Week 7

lush

mitigate

"The difference between try and
triumph is just a little umph!"
- Marvin Phillips

adj.

verb

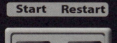

Start   Restart

1.
lithe
adj.

bending readily; pliant; limber; supple; flexible

Her naturally lithe physique made her a great dancer.

2.
litigate
v.

to cause to become the subject-matter of a suit at law.

She wanted to litigate the matter in court.

3.
livid
adj.

pale and ashen; black-and-blue, as contused flesh; extremely angry

David became livid with rage when he saw how Felicia had damaged his car in the careless accident.

4.
loathe
v.

to dislike greatly; abhor

I loathe seeing birds trapped in cages.

5.
lobby
v.

to try to influence the thinking of legislators for or against a specific cause

Special interest groups lobby senators and congressmen in order to get legislation passed to favor certain groups.

6.
lout
n.

an awkward and stupid person; an oaf; a boor

It was no surprise that the loud had made such a scene at the restaurant, demanding that his food be brought before anyone else's in the eatery.

7.
lucid
adj.

easily understood; completely intelligible or comprehensible

The policy was hardly lucid; everyone who read the first sentence walked away completely confused about its meaning.

8.
lukewarm
adj.

unenthusaistic; mildly warm

There was only lukewarm reception for our show, so the ticket sales were mediocre at best.

9.

lull

n.

a period of relative inactivity or calm

The storm came to a lull, so the animal came out of hiding.

10.

luminous

adj.

giving or radiating light

The luminous midnight moon provided light for the grave robbers at the cemetery.

11.

lurid

adj.

ghastly and sensational

The tabloids are filled with lurid tales of deception, romance, and death.

12.

lush

adj.

having or characterized by luxuriant vegetation; abundant; plentiful

The lush vegetable garden could provide the family with food for the entire winter.

13.

lustrous

adj.

shining

The lustrous pearl, perfect and shiny, would have fetched thousands of dollars.

14.

luxurious

adj.

characterized by rich or extravagant variety

She sat in the bathtub with candles around the tub, soaking in a luxurious bubble bath.

15.

magnanimous adj.

noble and generous in spirit; forgiving and free from petty resentfulness

Mrs. Gallagher was magnanimous when she gave tens of thousands of dollars to the orphanage.

16.

malcontent

n.

one who is dissatisfied with the existing state of affairs

Josie was a notorious malcontent in her family, for she was never satisfied with the way things were.

WEEK 1
WEEK 2
WEEK 3
WEEK 4
WEEK 5
WEEK 6
WEEK 7
WEEK 8
WEEK 9
WEEK 10

REGULAR

17.

malevolent adj.

wishing evil or harm to another or others; showing ill will; ill-disposed; malicious

Those people are quite malevolent, wanting to make every child who comes near their park cry.

18.

malicious adj.

full of, characterized by, or showing hate; spiteful

His malicious attacks did nothing to help his reputation for being cruel.

19.

malignancy n.

the quality or condition of being extremely harmful

She wanted to study cancers because she was fascinated by the malignancy of tumors.

20.

malleable adj.

capable of being extended or shaped

Gold is very valuable partly because of its malleable nature, capable of being shaped into priceless jewelry.

21.

mammoth adj.

immensely large; huge; enormous

That mountain that looms before us is mammoth; it must tower at least 10,000 feet.

22.

manifold adj.

of many kinds; numerous and varied; (n.) something having many different parts or features

He gave up for manifold reasons, none of which stood out as the most significant.

23.

mar v.

to inflict damage, especially disfiguring damage

Our wonderful holiday break was marred by terrible weather.

24.

maverick n.

one that refuses to abide by the dictates of or resists adherence to a group; a dissenter

The engineer was a maverick, often coming up with unique methods of construction.

25.

maxim
n.

an expression of a general truth or principle

The maxims from Aesop's fables have become an important part of Western folklore.

26.

meander
v.

to wind and turn while proceeding in a course

The stream meandered down the mountains, through the valley, and into the sea.

27.

mediate
v.

to settle (disputes, strikes, etc.) as an intermediary between parties; reconcile

A counselor was brought in to mediate between the students to help resolve their problems.

28.

mediocre
adj.

ordinary

Because Shelly was such an obedient child at home, her parents did not bother her about her mediocre grades.

29.

meditate
v.

to engage in thought or contemplation; reflect

I love to sit at the end of the pier and meditate on life while I look out over the vast, endless sea.

30.

melancholy
adj.

affected with, characterized by, or showing melancholy; mournful; depressed; (n.) a gloomy state of mind, esp. when habitual or prolonged; depression

She felt so melancholy, sad and gloomy after her dog had run away from home.

31.

mellifluous
adj.

having a smooth and sweetly flowing sound

Pedro wooed Rosalinda with his mellifluous serenades.

32.

metamorphosis n.

a passing from one form or shape into another

The metamorphosis of a caterpillar to a butterfly was interesting to the 4th grade class.

WEEK 1
WEEK 2
WEEK 3
WEEK 4
WEEK 5
WEEK 6
WEEK 7
WEEK 8
WEEK 9
WEEK 10

REGULAR

33.
metaphor   n.

a figure of speech in which a term or phrase is applied to something to which it is not literally applicable in order to suggest a resemblance

She saw success as a staircase, a metaphor for a continuous effort to climb to the top of her field.

34.
migrate   v.

to go from one country, region, or place to another

Farm workers often migrate from field to field to earn money during harvest season.

35.
mime   n.

the art or technique of portraying a character, mood, idea, or narration by gestures and bodily movement; the person who performs this art; (v.) to mimic

I love to watch the mime present the story of Goldilocks simply with his hand and body motions.

36.
minute   adj.

extremely small, as in size, amount, extent, or degree

Plankton, a minute life form, can be seen only under a microscope.

37.
mirth   n.

gladness and gaiety, especially when expressed by laughter

The excitement and the mirth of a holiday season makes two weeks go by quickly.

38.
misconstrue   v.

to mistake the meaning of; misinterpret

The lawyer misconstrued his client's views, making it very difficult for him to provide adequate defense.

39.
miserly   adj.

of, like, or befitting a miser; stingy

Ebeneezer Scrooge acted miserly even at Christmas time, refusing to give a penny to help the poor.

40.
misnomer   n.

a name wrongly or mistakenly applied

To call Native Americans "Indians" is a misnomer; they are not from India.

41.

mitigate   v.

to make milder or more endurable

Though medication will mitigate the pain, they will not eliminate it completely.

42.

mollify   v.

to soothe

Delilah was able to mollify her rambunctious puppy with a chew toy.

43.

monolith   n.

a large block of stone used in a structure; anything suggestive of a large block of stone

The designers of the monument made a monolith, something massive enough to commemorate the gravity of the battle.

44.

monologue   n.

a story or drama told or performed by one person

We went to see the comedian at the comedy club and laughed throughout his opening monologue.

45.

monotonous   adj.

lacking in variety; tediously unvarying

No one wanted to listen to the radio program because the guest host spoke in a dull, monotonous manner.

46.

morale   n.

the degree of confidence and optimism of a group or person, esp. in regard to discipline and the willingness to perform assigned tasks

Troops fought even harder when their colonel boosted their morale with stories of glorious victory.

47.

moronic   adj.

displaying the characteristic of a person who is notably stupid or lacking in good judgement

I called his plan idiotic and he said mine was moronic!

48.

morose   adj.

gloomily ill-humored, as a person or mood

I noticed that lately you have been very morose after coming from home; I certainly hope you and your wife are no longer fighting.

WEEK 1
WEEK 2
WEEK 3
WEEK 4
WEEK 5
WEEK 6
WEEK 7
WEEK 8
WEEK 9
WEEK 10

REGULAR

49.
mortify
v.

to cause to experience shame, humiliation, or wounded pride

She was mortified to find out that her dogs had destroyed her neighbor's prize-winning rose bush.

50.
mosaic
n.

a picture or design made by setting small pieces of tile or stone into a surface

Martha was fond of the process of breaking old pottery into bits to make her beautiful mosaics.

51.
mottled
adj.

spotted or blotched by different shades or colors

The jockey knew that the mottled horse would do well in the next race.

52.
mull
v.

to study; ponder

Before he said yes, he had to mull over all his other options.

53.
mundane
adj.

of or pertaining to this world or earth as contrasted with heaven; worldly; earthly; common

The movie, *Little Women*, is about the mundane lives of the Alcott sisters.

54.
munificence
n.

a giving characterized by generous motives and extraordinary liberality

Bill Gates has given millions of dollars to education and is highly regarded for this munificence.

55.
muse
v.

to become absorbed in one's thoughts; engage in meditation

The sad student mused about his future, hoping somehow to find peace in his life.

56.
muster
adj.

to call together; to summon or gather; to call forth an inner quality, such as strength

The police are mustering the tactical team to strike against the terrorists hiding out in the old warehouse.

57.

mutable

adj.

liable or subject to change or alteration

Many viruses are difficult to cure since they are quite mutable, never remaining in their original form.

58.

mutilate

v.

to disfigure

A piece of cake left to the hands of a baby will often be mutilated in the process of being eaten.

59.

myth

n.

a traditional or legendary story, usually concerning some being or hero or event, with or without a determinable basis of fact or a natural explanation

Greek myth is filled with stories about complex relationships among the gods.

60.

nagging

adj.

persistently bothersome; continually faultfinding; complaining

I have this nagging cough that doesn't seem to let me do much during the day.

61.

naïve

adj.

having or showing a lack of experience, judgment, or information; gullible or easily persuaded

Elaine was well loved, but she was so naïve, believing that such a scoundrel as Ernest could be her true love.

62.

nauseous

adj.

causing nausea; sickening

I thought I was going to throw up after smelling the nauseous scent of the skunk.

63.

nefarious

adj.

infamous because of extreme wickedness; evil

The Zodiac Killer's nefarious deeds held the Bay Area in a state of suspended fear.

64.

negligence

n.

omission of that which ought to be done

Failing his Spanish final, he realized, he could blame nothing more than his own negligence.

WEEK 1
WEEK 2
WEEK 3
WEEK 4
WEEK 5
WEEK 6
WEEK 7
WEEK 8
WEEK 9
WEEK 10

REGULAR

65.

negligible   adj.

not significant or important enough to be worth considering

The money left over after the purchase of the new entertainment system was negligible.

66.

nemesis   n.

one's primary enemy

Little did he know that the office manager had sworn herself to be his greatest nemesis and would do everything in her power to destroy him.

67.

nestle   v.

to adjust cozily in snug quarters

The children were nestled in their beds after a long day of fun at Sea World.

68.

neurotic   adj.

relating to a nervous or emotional disorder; overanxious

The woman who suffers from the neurotic fixation cannot stop checking her watch to see if she's late.

69.

nimble   adj.

light and quick in motion or action

Jack was so nimble that he easily jumped over the car.

70.

nomadic   adj.

moving from place to place

Nomadic tribes are constantly on the move, sometimes in search of fresh grazing land for their livestock.

71.

nostalgia   n.

desire to return in thought or in fact to a former time in one's life, to one's home or homeland, or to one's family and friends; a sentimental yearning for the happiness of a former place or time

Most older people, when they hear a song from their youth, go into a state of nostalgia, reliving the memories of where they were when that song first appeared.

72.

notoriety   n.

the state, quality, or character of being notorious or widely known

Gangsters achieved notoriety during Prohibition as they operated illegal, yet colorful, smuggling rings around the country.

73.

noxious adj.

harmful or injurious to health or physical well-being

A noxious odor from the chemical plant filled the rooms of the school, forcing the principal to cut classes for the day.

74.

obdurate adj.

unmoved by persuasion, pity, or tender feelings; stubborn; unyielding

Freddie remained obdurate, unwilling to budge even when his youngest daughter pleaded not to be sent to her room.

75.

obligate v.

to hold to the fulfillment of duty

Oscar hoped that he might obligate Celia to let him use her stereo if he bought her some of her favorite CDs.

76.

oppress v.

to burden with cruel or unjust impositions or restraints; subject to a burdensome or harsh exercise of authority or power

In the conquered country, the peasants were oppressed by the invaders, sent to concentration camps and virtually starved to death.

77.

optimistic adj.

disposed to take a favorable view of events or conditions and to expect the most favorable outcome

You should not be so optimistic about going to an Ivy League school if you have a D average in school.

78.

opulence n.

wealth, riches, or affluence

Cities like Beverly Hills and San Marino are noted for having houses that show the residents' opulence.

79.

ornery adj.

ugly and unpleasant in disposition or temper

Jeff acted rather ornery when he was told he couldn't go out until his homework was finished.

80.

oscillate v.

to swing or move to and fro, as a pendulum does

The physicist kept a close eye on the computer analysis of the light waves as they oscillated between red and orange.

WEEK 1
WEEK 2
WEEK 3
WEEK 4
WEEK 5
WEEK 6
WEEK 7
WEEK 8
WEEK 9
WEEK 10

REGULAR

81.

ostentatious   adj.

characterized by or given to conspicuous show in an attempt to impress others

Having fifteen Statues of Liberty lining your driveway could qualify you as being a bit ostentatious.

82.

overwrought   adj.

excessively nervous or agitated; overdone

The young child was overwrought with the news that her dog had been hit by a car.

83.

pacify   v.

to bring into a peaceful state

The new mother could pacify her little baby with her sweetly sung lullabies.

84.

pagan   n.

one who is not a Christian, Muslim, or Jew; a worshiper of a polytheistic religion; one who has no religion

The Greeks were pagans who worshipped a number of gods, the chief of whom was Zeus.

85.

painstaking   adj.

requiring great pains; very careful and diligent

Jessica rendered each leaf of the tree in painstaking detail.

86.

palatable   adj.

acceptable to the taste

A bland meal can be made more palatable with the addition of soy sauce.

87.

palate   n.

sense of taste

The ten course meal was a delight to the palate.

88.

palatial   adj.

of the nature of a palace; expansive, huge

The Bellagio in Las Vegas is very palatial with its marble floors and huge swimming pools.

89.

palliate

v.

to relieve or lessen without curing; alleviate

The lawyer's proof of that the defendant had a reasonable motive for his crime palliated the judge's sentence to community service.

90.

pandemic

adj.

affecting a whole people or all classes, as a disease

Starvation has reached almost pandemic proportions because of worldwide drought.

91.

panorama

n.

a series of large pictures representing a continuous scene

The house on the cliff had a full panorama of the mountains and the sea.

92.

paradigm

n.

an example serving as a model; pattern

New York is the paradigm of a modern metropolis.

93.

paragon

n.

a model of excellence

An Olympic athlete is a paragon of determination and strength.

94.

paramour

n.

an secret lover, esp. of a married person

Mr. Smith's divorce came when his wife had discovered that he had several paramours over the year.

95.

pariah

n.

an outcast

The new student, a pariah, was disliked by all who knew him.

96.

parody

n.

a humorous or satirical imitation of a serious piece of literature or writing; (v.) to imitate for purposes of ridicule or satire

"Weird Al" Yankovic composes parodies of popular songs, such as taking the song "Gangsta's Paradise" and turning it to "Amish Paradise."

WEEK 1
WEEK 2
WEEK 3
WEEK 4
WEEK 5
WEEK 6
WEEK 7
WEEK 8
WEEK 9
WEEK 10

REGULAR

97.

partisan n.

an adherent or supporter of a person, group, party, or cause, esp. a person who shows a biased, emotional allegiance; (adj.) partial to a specific party, person, etc.

The campaign was marred by excessive partisan bickering.

98.

pastoral adj.

having the spirit or sentiment of rural life; relating to a pastor or his duties

She longed for pastoral landscapes buzzing with insects and humming with birds.

99.

pathos n.

the quality in any form of representation that rouses emotion or sympathy

Whether poetry should express pathos is a subject of controversy among contemporary poets.

100.

patronage n.

the financial support or business provided to a store, hotel, or the like, by customers, clients, or paying guests

The artist could spend all her time working on her painting because her finances were supported from the patronage of willing benefactors.

A. Fill in the appropriate words using the clues below.

across:

5) n. a giving characterized by generous motives and extraordinary liberality
6) adj. easily understood; completely intelligible or comprehensible
7) adj. ordinary
9) v. to relieve or lessen without curing; mitigate; alleviate

down:

1) n. desire to return in thought or in fact to a former time in one's life
2) adj. liable or subject to change or alteration
3) v. to soothe
4) n. wealth, riches, or affluence
5) adj. extremely small, as in size, amount, extent, or degree
8) adj. unmoved by persuasion, pity, or tender feelings; stubborn; unyielding

B. Match the words on the left with their appropriate definitions on the right.

A. livid _____ 1. adj. immensely large; huge; enormous

B. magnanimous _____ 2. v. to swing or move to and fro, as a pendulum does

C. malevolent _____ 3. adj. wishing evil or harm to another or others; showing ill will; ill-disposed; malicious

D. malicious _____ 4. adj. harmful or injurious to health or physical well-being

E. mammoth _____ 5. adj. having or showing a lack of experience, judgment, or information; gullible; easily persuaded

F. maverick _____ 6. adj. pale and ashen; black-and-blue, as contused flesh; extremely angry

G. miserly _____ 7. adj. noble and generous in spirit; forgiving and free from petty resentfulness

H. mitigate _____ 8. n. one's primary enemy

I. morose _____ 9. adj. having the spirit or sentiment of rural life; relating to a pastor or his duties

J. mundane _____ 10. adj. acceptable to the taste

K. naïve _____ 11. adj. full of, characterized by, or showing hate; spiteful

L. nefarious _____ 12. n. one that refuses to abide by the dictates of or resists adherence to a group; a dissenter

M. nemesis _____ 13. adj. infamous because of extreme wickedness; evil

N. noxious _____ 14. n. an example serving as a model; pattern

O. oscillate _____ 15. v. to make milder or more endurable

P. ostentatious _____ 16. n. a model of excellence

Q. palatable _____ 17. adj. of or pertaining to this world or earth as contrasted with heaven; worldly; common

R. paradigm _____ 18. adj. gloomily ill-humored, as a person or mood

S. paragon _____ 19. adj. of, like, or befitting a miser; stingy

T. pastoral _____ 20. adj. characterized by or given to conspicuous show in an attempt to impress others

Week 8

100pts

300pts

pious

pretext

adj.

noun

"Desire is the key to motivation, but it's
determination and commitment to an
unrelenting pursuit of your goal--
a commitment to excellence--
that will enable you to attain
the success you seek."
- Mario Andretti

1.
patronizing
adj.

displaying or indicative of an offensively condescending manner

Her boss would often speak to her in such a patronizing manner that she felt she had to ask his permission to go out on the weekends.

2.
paucity
n.

smallness of number; scarcity

A paucity of kindness will lead to an abundance of suffering.

3.
pauper
n.

one without means of support

The man became a pauper because he suddenly got sick, could not work, and had overwhelming doctor bills to pay.

4.
peddle
v.

to go about with a small stock of goods to sell

The man peddled his homemade remedies to naïve customers at the country fair.

5.
pedestrian
adj.

lacking vitality, imagination, or distinction; commonplace

Critics dismissed the novel as another pedestrian effort for the mediocre writer.

6.
pedigree
n.

one's line of ancestors; the line of descent of a purebred animal

The pedigree of the Kent family's cocker spaniels was verified by the American Kennel Society.

7.
peevish
adj.

cross, irritable, or fretful, as from discontent

Dr. Quincy often treated his patients poorly, acting rather peevish from their constant physical complaints.

8.
penance
n.

punishment to which one voluntarily submits or subjects himself as an expression of regret

Writing that he would not tattle on his classmates 100 times was the penance Aaron had to pay for his misdeeds.

WEEK 1
WEEK 2
WEEK 3
WEEK 4
WEEK 5
WEEK 6
WEEK 7
WEEK 8
WEEK 9
WEEK 10

REGULAR

9.

penchant n.

a strong inclination, taste, or liking for something

The boys had a penchant for mischief that often got them into trouble with the principal.

10.

penitence n.

sorrow for sin with desire to amend and to atone

Pilgrims may travel for miles on hands and knees to show penitence for their sins.

11.

pensive adj.

dreamily or wistfully thoughtful

Terry stood at the end of the pier with a pensive look on his face because he felt trapped in his new job away from his family.

12.

perforate v.

to make a hole or holes through

Because the paper has a perforated edge, it is easy to tear it out of the notebook.

13.

perilous adj.

involving or full of grave risk or peril; hazardous; dangerous

Climbing a cliff without the proper equipment is a perilous venture.

14.

permeate v.

to pass into or through every part of

The spilled ink permeated her brand new skirt.

15.

pernicious adj.

intending to hurt or cause severe harm

Julia admitted to having told a pernicious lie about her sister's involvement with Lou.

16.

pert adj.

boldly forward in speech or behavior; saucy; somewhat rude

Cassie came across to many as pert, often too opinionated for her own good.

17.

pertinent   adj.

relevant

Hugo revised his long essay on fruit beetles to include only the most pertinent details of their mating behavior.

18.

perturb   v.

to disturb greatly

The crack in the ceiling perturbs the family every time there is a rainstorm.

19.

perturbation   n.

mental excitement or confusion

The fourth graders caused Mr. Garrison such tremendous perturbation that he was forced to punish them with detention and Saturday school.

20.

pervade   v.

to pass or spread through every part

Stupidity and fear pervade most violent societies.

21.

pervasive   adj.

thoroughly penetrating or permeating

The pervasive use of anti-depressants in the U.S. has caused concern among moral and religious thinkers.

22.

perversion   n.

diversion from the true meaning or proper purpose

His version of the story is a gross perversion of the truth.

23.

pessimistic   adj.

pertaining to or characterized by pessimism; gloomy

With last quarter's profits as low as they were, we are rather pessimistic about our chances of keeping within our budget this year.

24.

petite   adj.

short and having a small, trim figure; diminutive

The hat was cute and petite, a small, frilly accessory to her colorful outfit.

WEEK 1
WEEK 2
WEEK 3
WEEK 4
WEEK 5
WEEK 6
WEEK 7
WEEK 8
WEEK 9
WEEK 10

REGULAR

25.
philanthropy n.

altruistic concern for human welfare and advancement, usually manifested by donations of money, property, or work to needy persons, by endowment of institutions of learning and hospitals, and by generosity to other socially useful purposes

The board approved a $100,000 contribution to the hospital, one of its most charitable acts of philanthropy this year.

26.
phobia n.

persistent, abnormal, or irrational fear of a specific thing or situation that compels one to avoid it

Candace needed quite a bit of therapy to rid herself of various phobias she had held since her childhood.

27.
pictorial adj.

pertaining to, expressed in, or of the nature of a picture

The movie successfully portrayed a pictorial rendition of the Battle of Gettysburg.

28.
picturesque adj.

visually charming or quaint, as if resembling or suitable for a painting

Kenttown was a small village nestled in the picturesque mountain setting.

29.
pious adj.

having or showing a dutiful spirit of reverence for God or an earnest wish to fulfill religious obligations

Each Sunday during mass, young Samuel attempted to imitate his father's pious expression.

30.
pique v.

to excite; provoke; arouse an emotional response

The new teacher piqued the students' interest in literature.

31.
pithy adj.

brief, forceful, and meaningful in expression; full of vigor, substance, or meaning; terse; forcible

I like when Joe speaks; he doesn't drag his ideas out but presents them in a short, pithy form.

32.
placate v.

to bring from a state of angry or hostile feeling to one of patience or friendliness

Lennie was able to placate his angry father by promising to mow the lawn for the rest of his life.

33.

placid adj.

calm; undisturbed

After the rough seas of the night before, Captain Stubing was relieved to wake to placid waters and clear skies.

34.

plausible adj.

seeming likely to be true, though open to doubt

A plausible alibi made the suspect seem more trustworthy.

35.

plenitude n.

abundance

There is a plenitude of food left on the table for her five sons to eat.

36.

plethora n.

overabundance; excess

A plethora of ideas came out of the brainstorming session for selling the new soft drink.

37.

pliable adj.

easily bent or shaped

The pliable metal sheets were easily pounded into interesting shapes.

38.

plight n.

an unfortunate situation or circumstance

Joseph found himself in a sorry plight when his father caught him stealing his mother's jewelry.

39.

plummet v.

to fall straight down; plunge

The man plummeted 50 feet to his death after climbing on the rocks.

40.

pneumatic adj.

pertaining to or consisting of air or gas

We had to use a pneumatic drill to complete the job.

WEEK 1
WEEK 2
WEEK 3
WEEK 4
WEEK 5
WEEK 6
WEEK 7
WEEK 8
WEEK 9
WEEK 10

REGULAR

41.

poignant   adj.

severely painful or acute to the spirit

Her poignant letter brought tears to her mother's eyes.

42.

poise   n.

demonstrating composure; the state of being emotionally, as well as physically balanced

The new manager demonstrated great poise on her first day, creating a healthy and productive workplace.

43.

polarize   v.

to cause a group to separate into two conflicting or contrasting positions

Hillary Clinton polarized the American voters; people seemed either to love her or to hate her.

44.

politic   adj.

shrewd or prudent in practical matters; tactful; diplomatic

To negotiate between two sides so antagonistic to each other will require a very politic approach.

45.

pompous   adj.

marked by an assumed stateliness and impressiveness of manner; arrogant

After graduating with the highest honors, Hugh became rather pompous about his accomplishments.

46.

ponderous   adj.

lacking fluency; dull and serious; having great weight or bulk

While her prose is rather ponderous, her claims are quite sound.

47.

portent   n.

anything that indicates what is to happen

The teacher's cryptic portent indicated that there would be a surprise exam the following week.

48.

posterity   n.

future generations

Jenny wanted to leave something beneficial to posterity, so she decided to write down her family history.

49.

posthumous   adj.

occurring or continuing after one's death

The new book is a posthumous publication, derived from an unfinished manuscript found shortly after the author's death.

50.

postulate   v.

to make a claim for; to assume or assert the truth

Mr. Bigsley postulates that because his son has grown quite thin in recent months, he must not be eating lunch at school.

51.

potent   adj.

physically powerful

Coffee has long been known to be a potent stimulant.

52.

prattle   v.

to talk in a foolish or simple-minded way; chatter; babble

No matter what he did, Brian could not stop her from prattling on about her many pets.

53.

precarious   adj.

potentially dangerous; uncertain; unstable; insecure

The giant crack in the center of the bridge left the structure in a precarious state.

54.

precept   n.

a commandment or direction given as a rule of action or conduct

The king expected the court to obey his new precepts addressing proper respect to the king.

55.

precipice   n.

a high and very steep or approximately vertical cliff

The mountain climber summited the dangerous precipice.

56.

precipitate   v.

to force forward prematurely; to cause to happen, especially suddenly or prematurely

Economists warn that printing more money will precipitate inflation and eventual economic disaster.

WEEK 1
WEEK 2
WEEK 3
WEEK 4
WEEK 5
WEEK 6
WEEK 7
WEEK 8
WEEK 9
WEEK 10

REGULAR

57.

precocious   adj.

being intelligent or otherwise developed at a young age

We found out how precocious Trevor was when, at the age of five, he began composing epic poetry.

58.

precursor   n.

a forerunner or herald

The first robin you see is a precursor of spring.

59.

predicament   n.

a difficult, trying situation or plight

Because of her hatred of snails, Francesca found herself in quite a predicament when her garden was overrun by them.

60.

predicate   v.

to base on a cause; to attribute

The stock market crash was predicated on years of irresponsible lending and investor speculation.

61.

preeminent   adj.

superior or notable above all others

It is the goal of most scholars to become preeminent in their fields.

62.

preempt   v.

to take the place of; to occur before something else; take for oneself; interrupt

The baseball game was preempted so that a special news report could be broadcast.

63.

preface   n.

a brief explanation or address to the reader, at the beginning of a book

The preface of the book was written by the author's very good friend.

64.

prelude   n.

an introductory or opening performance

His symphony begins with a delightful prelude intended to lull the audience before the first movement.

65.
premeditated   adj.

planned, arranged, or plotted in advance

Premeditated murder is considered to be the most heinous of crimes.

66.
premise   n.

a proposition which is assumed to be true and which an argument or conclusion is based on

A syllogism is a logical formulation that consists of two premises and one conclusion.

67.
preoccupation   n.

absorption of the attention or intellect

His preoccupation with insects led him to select entomology as his major in college.

68.
preordain   v.

to determine in advance

That little Johnny wouldn't play in the NBA was almost preordained; alas, he was only four feet, eight inches tall.

69.
prerogative   n.

having superior rank or precedence

It was the teacher's prerogative to stop the discussion before it turned to more lurid subjects.

70.
presage   v.

to foretell

Do you think the appearance of the knife on the countertop presages a murder?

71.
prestige   n.

reputation or influence arising from success, achievement, rank, or other favorable attributes

Teaching math and science grew in prestige after the government allocated millions of dollars to military and industrial research.

72.
presumption   n.

that which may be logically assumed to be true until disproved

The presumption that talent is paramount is false; hard work is the true key to achieving success.

WEEK 1
WEEK 2
WEEK 3
WEEK 4
WEEK 5
WEEK 6
WEEK 7
WEEK 8
WEEK 9
WEEK 10

REGULAR

73.
presuppose
v.

to believe or suppose in advance

The teacher presupposed the students' understanding of the material and skipped many chapters.

74.
pretension
n.

a bold or presumptuous assertion

My friends laughed at my pretensions to more moral behavior.

75.
pretext
n.

a fictitious reason or motive

The boys used the insults as a pretext for a fight.

76.
prevalence
n.

the quality of being widespread or common

The song's prevalence on the radio reflects its great popularity.

77.
prim
adj.

stiffly proper

Although Mrs. Forester was normally quite prim, she did like to disco dance.

78.
pristine
adj.

remaining in a pure state; uncorrupted by civilization

Few truly pristine old growth forests remain on Earth today.

79.
probation
n.

a process or period of time during which a person's character or qualifications are tested

The new employees had to work through a six-week period of probation before the company would provide benefits.

80.
prodigal
adj.

wastefully or recklessly extravagant

The story of the prodigal son relates a father's forgiveness toward a son who has foolishly spent all his wealth.

81.

prodigious adj.

extraordinary in size, amount, extent, degree, force, etc.

I couldn't believe I made a prodigious amount from such a small investment.

82.

prodigy n.

a person or thing of very remarkable gifts or qualities

The child prodigy received a Nobel Prize in physics at the age of 16.

83.

profane adj.

showing contempt or irreverence for what is sacred; vulgar; blasphemous

We encourage lively discussion, but ask you to refrain from racist, abusive, or profane comments.

84.

proficient adj.

well-advanced or competent in any art, science, or subject; skilled

A good diplomat must be proficient in the language and culture of the people with whom he must interact.

85.

profound adj.

penetrating or entering deeply into subjects of thought or knowledge; having deep insight or understanding

I have a profound respect for you since you have helped so many members of my family.

86.

profuse adj.

produced or displayed in overabundance

The profuse amount of tissues used for her running nose filled the trash bin.

87.

proliferate v.

to grow or reproduce; to spread rapidly

Rats began to proliferate throughout the city, causing great concern among the residents.

88.

prolific adj.

reproducing abundantly; producing many works of art

Hamsters and rabbits are prolific pets; after only one year, an owner could be overwhelmed by the duties of caring for their offspring.

WEEK 1
WEEK 2
WEEK 3
WEEK 4
WEEK 5
WEEK 6
WEEK 7
WEEK 8
WEEK 9
WEEK 10

REGULAR

89.

promulgate   v.

to proclaim

The lieutenant colonel promulgated the order among his troops that no one was to mistreat the prisoners of war.

90.

prone   adj.

having a natural inclination or tendency to something

When the Origin of the Species came out, the scientific community embraced Darwin's views and propagated his conclusions about natural selection.

91.

propagate   v.

to spread from person to person; to reproduce

It is a shame that some people propagate hatred on websites such as Facebook or MySpace.

92.

propensity   n.

tendency

Josey's propensity for critical analysis proved useful to her major in philosophy.

93.

propitious   adj.

presenting favorable conditions; favorable

The anxious beachgoers are excited about the propitious weather that is about to come their way.

94.

propriety   n.

accordance with recognized usage, custom, or principles

The village leaders insisted that the rules of propriety be maintained throughout the controversial trial.

95.

prosaic   adj.

unimaginative

While her poetry was formally quite inventive, its subject matter was rather prosaic.

96.

prose   n.

the ordinary form of spoken or written language, without metrical structure, as distinguished from poetry or verse

The talented author won many literary awards that recognized his skill with prose.

97.

prosperous   adj.

characterized by material abundance; lucrative

Father ran a quite prosperous cigar shop before deciding to search for rare butterflies full time.

98.

prostrate   adj.

lying prone, or with the head to the ground

The knight fell to the ground in servitude, prostrate before his queen.

99.

protagonist   n.

a leader in any enterprise or contest

The protagonist of every story usually goes through a transformation of character.

100.

prototype   n.

a work, original in character, afterward imitated in form or spirit

The prototype of the new electric sports car is amazing, not only in speed but also in style.

A. Fill in the appropriate words using the clues below.

across:

2) adj. penetrating or entering deeply into subjects of thought or knowledge; having deep insight or understanding
6) n. a bold or presumptuous assertion
7) v. to base on a cause; to attribute
9) n. a strong inclination, taste, or liking for something

down:

1) n. tendency
3) adj. intending to hurt or cause severe harm
4) adj. dreamily or wistfully thoughtful
5) adj. physically powerful
6) adj. having a superior rank or precedence
8) v. to bring from a state of angry or hostile feeling to one of patience or friendliness

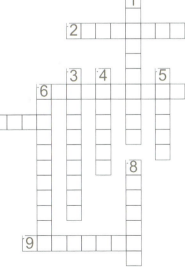

WEEK 1
WEEK 2
WEEK 3
WEEK 4
WEEK 5
WEEK 6
WEEK 7
WEEK 8
WEEK 9
WEEK 10
REGULAR

B. Match the words on the left with their appropriate definitions on the right.

A. paucity _____

B. pernicious _____

C. pertinent _____

D. pervasive _____

E. pious _____

F. placid _____

G. plethora _____

H. poignant _____

I. poise _____

J. pompous _____

K. precarious _____

L. precocious _____

M. preempt _____

N. premise _____

O. prestige _____

P. prim _____

Q. prodigy _____

R. proliferate _____

S. prosaic _____

T. prototype _____

1. v. to take the place of; to occur before something else; take for oneself; interrupt

2. adj. relevant

3. n. demonstrating composure; the state of being emotionally, as well as physically balanced

4. n. a proposition which is assumed to be true and which an argument or conclusion is based on

5. adj. marked by an assumed stateliness and impressiveness of manner; arrogant

6. n. reputation or influence arising from success, achievement, rank, or other favorable attributes

7. adj. unimaginative

8. n. smallness of number; scarcity

9. v. to grow or reproduce; to spread rapidly

10. adj. intending to hurt or cause severe harm

11. adj. thoroughly penetrating or permeating

12. adj. potentially dangerous; uncertain; unstable; insecure

13. n. overabundance; excess

14. n. a work, original in character, afterward imitated in form or spirit

15. adj. having or showing a dutiful spirit of reverence for God

16. adj. calm; undisturbed

17. n. a person or thing of very remarkable gifts or qualities

18. adj. being intelligent or otherwise developed at a young age

19. adj. severely painful or acute to the spirit

20. adj. stiffly proper

300pts

100pts

Week 9

tacit

surfeit

"We are what we repeatedly do. Excellence, then, is not an act, but a habit."
- Aristotle

adj.

noun

Start   Restart

1.

protract
v.

to prolong

The meeting was protracted for hours because of lengthy excuses and finger pointing among the team members.

2.

protrude
v.

to push out or thrust forth

The loose nail protruded from the fence and posed a hazard, so we hammered it down.

3.

proverb
n.

a short popular saying, usually of unknown and ancient origin, that expresses effectively some commonplace truth or useful thought; adage; saw

His mother was remembered for the proverbs she would tell all her children and their friends, phrases they have lived by.

4.

provident
adj.

anticipating and making ready for future wants or emergencies

Mother's provident nature meant that we never ran out of supplies.

5.

provincial
adj.

unsophisitcated in thought and culture; limited in perspective

A number of the citizens of the small hamlet lived provincial lives, untouched by the city only 50 miles away.

6.

prowess
n.

strength, skill, and intrepidity in battle

Often the soldier boasted that his prowess had led him to battle so fiercely that he deserved the medals of bravery bestowed on him.

7.

proximally
adv.

occurring very near or next

She arranged the flowers according to color and texture, nestling the roses proximally to the fiddle sticks.

8.

prudence
n.

careful management; economy

Prudence in one's spending habits can help one to save money.

9.

pungent adj.

having a sharp or bitter smell or taste; to the point, penetrating

The pungent odors of the Indian curries assailed our noses, making us hungry for some rich and spicy food.

10.

punitive adj.

related to punishment

The teacher took punitive measures in order to convince her students that she could not be taken advantage of.

11.

querulous adj.

full of complaints; complaining

The kids sat in the back seat whining in a querulous manner about not being allowed to stop at the water park.

12.

quiescent adj.

being inactive or quiet

The quiescent gecko, resting silently on the rock, hoped to evade its predator.

13.

rail v.

to utter bitter complaint or vehement denunciation (often fol. by at or against)

Don railed at his brothers for not having done their chores when he had done all of his.

14.

rampant adj.

growing or occurring without restraint

The rampant growth of blackberry vines in our backyard seemed fortuitous at first, but now the thorny bushes have all but taken over.

15.

rancor n.

bitter, rankling resentment or ill will; hatred; malice

The two basketball teams competed so fiercely that after the game they had rancor for each other.

16.

rant v.

to speak for or against in a wild or vehement way; rave

He ranted on and on about how he hated the long lines at the grocery store.

WEEK 1
WEEK 2
WEEK 3
WEEK 4
WEEK 5
WEEK 6
WEEK 7
WEEK 8
WEEK 9
WEEK 10

REGULAR

17.
rash   adj.

acting or tending to act too hastily or
without due consideration

Don't be so rash in deciding where
you will go to college; check out
several different possible campuses.

18.
ravenous   adj.

extremely hungry; famished

Nathan was ravenous, so he went to
McDonald's and ate ten Big Macs in
half an hour.

19.
rebuke   v.

to express sharp, stern disapproval
of; reprove; reprimand; (n.) sharp,
stern disapproval; reprimand

The teacher rebuked the class for
their apathetic attitude toward a
lesson she felt should be life
changing.

20.
rebut   v.

to refute by evidence or argument

Debaters seek not only to promote
their points but to rebut the opposing
assertions to theirs.

21.
recalcitrant   adj.

resisting authority or control; not
obedient or compliant

She remained a recalcitrant witness,
refusing to give any additional
information that would either prove the
defendant's guilt or acquit him of all
charges.

22.
recluse   n.

one who lives in seclusion, voluntarily
separated from society

The recluse lived by himself in a cabin
far from town and only ventured out
once a month to buy groceries and
supplies.

23.
refute   v.

to prove to be false or erroneous, as
an opinion or charge

I want to refute the assertion that I am
always late; you just start meetings
earlier than scheduled.

24.
relegate   v.

to send or consign to an inferior
position, place, or condition

Because of his C, Martin was
relegated to a lower English
composition class.

25.

reminiscent adj.

awakening memories of something
similar; suggestive

The perfume was reminiscent of the scent of lilacs he had smelled growing up.

26.

render v.

to cause to be or become; make

The jury rendered a guilty verdict at the trial of the music producer.

27.

rendezvous n.

a prearranged place of meeting (or
the meeting itself).

Our rendezvous had been planned for months--we were to meet at our favorite restaurant-- but for some reason he didn't show up.

28.

repress v.

to keep under control, check, or
suppress (desires, feelings, actions,
tears, etc.)

The team repressed their sadness at the loss of their coach and vowed to win the championship that year in his honor.

29.

reprimand v.

to criticize severely; (n.) a severe
reproof or rebuke, esp. a formal one
by a person in authority

Dalia would reprimand Mark constantly for his lazy attitude and poor work habits.

30.

reprove v.

to criticize or correct, esp. gently

We should reprove anyone who tries to tell us that we cannot succeed at such an easy goal as this.

31.

repudiate v.

to reject as having no authority or
binding force

The Bards repudiated their membership to the country club because it would not allow anyone who was not white to join.

32.

resolve v.

to come to a definite or earnest
decision about; determine (to do
something)

I resolve to complete my work by 8 PM tonight.

WEEK 1
WEEK 2
WEEK 3
WEEK 4
WEEK 5
WEEK 6
WEEK 7
WEEK 8
WEEK 9
WEEK 10

REGULAR

33.

restrain

v.

to hold back from action; keep in check or under control

Try to restrain yourself from speaking at the funeral; it is more an occasion for silence and respect for the deceased.

34.

reticent

adj.

habitually keeping silent or being reserved

Ever since his father died, the boy had been quite reticent, rarely speaking to anyone except for his dog.

35.

retrospective

adj.

directed to the past; contemplative of past situations, events

Before 2000, most TV stations aired a retrospective program about events of the 20th century.

36.

revere

v.

to regard with respect tinged with awe

You should revere police and firefighters since they are usually the first that you will see in any man-made or natural disaster.

37.

ruminate

v.

to meditate or muse; ponder

Facing a tough decision over who should win the prize, he ruminated over his various options for several hours before announcing his final choice.

38.

ruthless

adj.

without pity or compassion; cruel; merciless

Tyrants are ruthless in maintaining their power, taking great pains to eliminate any opposition to them whatsoever.

39.

sadistic

adj.

enjoying cruelty and the pain of others

Everyone worried about Darryl's sadistic tendencies with animals; he often trapped and tortured rabbits.

40.

saga

n.

any narrative or legend of heroic exploits

Early TV featured many shows that portrayed the sagas of the Old West.

41.

sanguine   adj.

cheerfully optimistic, hopeful, or confident

Such a sunny, warm day could make even the most pessimistic person far more sanguine about what the day may bring.

42.

sarcasm   n.

a sharply ironical taunt; sneering or cutting remark

Some of John's sarcasm could be quite biting and therefore hurtful.

43.

saturate   v.

to soak, impregnate, or imbue thoroughly or completely

After two weeks of steady rain, the fields were saturated, thus rendering them useless.

44.

saunter   v.

to walk with a leisurely gait; stroll

We should take the afternoon off, go to the woods, and saunter down the trails to the pond.

45.

savage   adj.

fierce, ferocious, or cruel; untamed; (n.) an uncivilized human being

Dr. Hitchcock stalked and killed the savage lion that had threatened the village.

46.

scenario   n.

an outline of the plot of a dramatic work, giving particulars as to the scenes, characters, situations, etc.

"Slumdog Millionaire" is set in a game show scenario much like "Who Wants To Be A Millionaire."

47

sedentary   adj.

characterized by or requiring a sitting posture

He had to break his sedentary habits of watching TV for 10 hours a day when he finally ran out of money for pretzels.

48.

seethe   v.

to overflow, be agitated

The customers were seething with anger when the waiter tripped and spilled a whole pitcher of water on them.

WEEK 1
WEEK 2
WEEK 3
WEEK 4
WEEK 5
WEEK 6
WEEK 7
WEEK 8
WEEK 9
WEEK 10

REGULAR

49.
segregate
v.

to separate or set apart from others or from the main body or group; isolate

No longer do we segregate people in the United States on the basis of race, gender, or religious beliefs.

50.
sentimental
adj.

expressive of or appealing to sentiment, esp. the tender emotions and feelings, as love, pity, or nostalgia

The card became a reflection of the sentimental value Andy held for his parents.

51.
sentinel
n.

any guard or watch stationed for protection

There are two sentinels standing by the front door of the prime minister's residence.

52.
serene
adj.

calm, peaceful, or tranquil

Lake Crater was known for its pristine, serene beauty.

53.
sermon
n.

a talk on a religious or moral subject; an often lengthy and tedious speech of reproof or exhortation

The sermon at the church addressed the moral crisis that erupted as the country contemplated war.

54.
shrewd
adj.

astute or sharp in practical matters

Someone looking for a new car should be shrewd when negotiating with dealers who want to make the highest commission possible on the sale.

55.
simulate
v.

to create a likeness, or model of (a situation, system, or the like)

Pilots must, periodically, simulate flight on the computer which places them in dangerous situations to test their knowledge and mental reflexes.

56.
singe
v.

to burn slightly or superficially

Diana's long hair was singed by the candle as she leaned over to eat her dinner.

57.

skeptical adj.

inclined to having strong doubt

Rita was skeptical about suggestions that old Mr. Barry's house was haunted.

58.

slander n.

defame by oral utterance rather than by writing, pictures, etc.

Because of the scathing rumors about their separation, the Emersons sued their neighbors, the Masons, for slander.

59.

sleight n.

a trick or feat so deftly done that the manner of performance escapes observation

Magicians use sleight of hand to perform card tricks.

60.

sluggish adj.

indisposed to action or exertion; lacking in energy; lazy

There's something wrong with this computer; it's acting sluggish, as though it needs about three days to boot up.

61.

sober adj.

temperate, more realistic

When the business collapsed in debt, Frank took a sober look at his assets and wondered whether it was worth it to start over.

62.

solemn adj.

grave, sober, or mirthless, as a person, the face, speech, tone, or mood

The church memorial service for the late judge was a solemn, reflective event.

63.

solvent adj.

able to pay all just debts; (n.) a substance that dissolves another to form a solution

Most banks are actually quite solvent; however, the recent economic crisis has tested the strength of many financial institutions.

64.

somnolent adj.

sleepy

I wonder why my cat is so somnolent; he sleeps for nearly seventeen hours out of every day.

WEEK 1
WEEK 2
WEEK 3
WEEK 4
WEEK 5
WEEK 6
WEEK 7
WEEK 8
WEEK 9
WEEK 10

REGULAR

65.
speculate v.

to engage in thought or reflection; meditate

I wanted to speculate on the stock market, but its downturn now has dissuaded me from doing so.

66.
spiteful adj.

full of spite or malice; showing spite; malicious; malevolent; venomous

In spite of my kindness to him, Gary remains spiteful each time we meet.

67.
sporadic adj.

appearing or happening at irregular intervals in time; occasional

The rain has not been consistent lately; we have had to deal with sporadic showers all week long.

68.
spurt v.

to gush or issue suddenly in a stream or jet, as a liquid; spout; (n.) a sudden, forceful gush or jet

He won the cross country race because of the spurt of energy he had over the last two hundred feet.

69.
stagnant adj.

inactive, sluggish, or dull

The stagnant water in the pond began to stink.

70.
static adj.

pertaining to or characterized by a fixed or stationary condition

No one made money last year because all investments were static, showing little, if any, growth.

71.
stipulate v.

to specify as a condition of agreement

The contract stipulated that all funds were to be transferred in the presence of a lawyer.

72.
stoic adj.

seemingly indifferent to or unaffected by pleasure or pain; impassive

The judge's countenance revealed a stoic demeanor, one not easily moved by pleading to his emotions.

73.

stratagem n.

a plan, scheme, or trick for surprising
or deceiving an enemy

Our stratagem for winning will be to
surround our opponents and then
move in to take over their territory.

74.

stupor n.

suspension or great diminution of
sensibility, as in disease or as caused
by narcotics, intoxicants, etc.

The auto accident left him in a stupor
from the sudden impact.

75.

suave adj.

smoothly agreeable or polite;
agreeably or blandly urbane

Caesar impressed everyone with his
suave Latin accent and mannerisms.

76.

subtle adj.

so slight as to be difficult to detect or
describe; elusive

Mike didn't take the subtle hint that he
really wasn't wanted at the pizza
parlor that night.

77.

succinct adj.

expressed in few words; concise;
terse

Keep your essays succinct; using
long, flowery sentences does not
mean that you have conveyed your
points.

78.

supercilious adj.

vainly disdainful or contemptuous, as
a person or a facial expression

Henrietta treated all those socially
below her in such a supercilious way
that even those who were her peers
grew uncomfortable with her attitude.

79.

superfluous adj.

being more than is sufficient or
required; excessive

Why they had to put that car chase
scene in the movie is beyond me; it
was a superfluous waste of 15
minutes.

80.

supervene v.

to take place or occur as something
additional or extraneous (sometimes
fol. by on or upon)

The tyrant supervened upon the
country laws that restricted movement
back and forth.

WEEK 1
WEEK 2
WEEK 3
WEEK 4
WEEK 5
WEEK 6
WEEK 7
WEEK 8
WEEK 9
WEEK 10

REGULAR

81.
suppress
v.

to do away with by or as if by authority; abolish; stop (a practice, custom, etc.)

They tried to suppress the evidence so that they could avoid a conviction.

82.
surfeit
n.

excess; an excessive amount

Oliver had a surfeit of books lying around his room, so avid was he a reader.

83.
surmount
v.

to overcome by force of will

If we truly apply ourselves, we can surmount this obstacle and be closer to realizing our dreams.

84.
swagger
v.

to walk or strut with a defiant or insolent air

Jimmy would swagger about down the street, refusing to acknowledge even a simple hello from any person who passed him by.

85.
sycophant
n.

a self-seeking, servile flatterer; fawning parasite

Joe is such a sycophant that the boss cannot go anywhere without Joe opening the door or carrying the boss' briefcase for him.

86.
synthesis
n.

the combining of the distinct elements of separate material or abstract entities into a single or unified entity

He was able to create a synthesis of the various ideas that answered the problems created by each assertion.

87.
tacit
adj.

understood

The general gave his tacit approval by giving a slight nod of his head; an explicit contract was not necessary.

88.
taciturn
adj.

inclined to silence; reserved in speech; reluctant to join in conversation

The naturally taciturn teenager rarely spoke, even when his opinion was wanted.

89.
tactful   adj.
having or showing a sense of what is fitting and considerate in dealing with others

I have to be very tactful with how I speak to Mary after she shaved her head in order to "make a statement."

90.
tactless   adj.
bluntly inconsiderate or indiscreet

The tactless baron asked about the countess's husband, who had died last month.

91.
taint   v.
to affect with or as if with a disease or decay

The spinach that sickened hundreds of consumers last year was tainted with E. coli bacteria.

92.
tally   n.
a mark used in recording a number of acts or objects, most often in series of five; (v.) to cause to correspond or agree

The tally for the school election was 450 to 250 in favor of Nora.

93.
tangential   adj.
merely touching or slightly connected; only superficially relevant; divergent

The lively speaker kept going off the original topic and making tangential, but amusing, remarks about other topics.

94.
taper   v.
to become gradually smaller or thinner at one end

An ice cream cone is round on top and tapers off to a small tip at the bottom.

95.
teem   v.
to be full to overflowing

The swamp water is teeming with bacteria, so make sure you keep your wound tightly wrapped as you wade across.

96.
temerity   n.
reckless boldness; rashness

I was shocked at his temerity when he stood up to his verbally abusive track coach.

WEEK 1
WEEK 2
WEEK 3
WEEK 4
WEEK 5
WEEK 6
WEEK 7
WEEK 8
WEEK 9
WEEK 10

REGULAR

97.
tenable
adj.

capable of being maintained in an
argument; rationally defensible

Newton's law of gravity is a tenable
theory.

98.
tenacious
adj.

holding tightly; characterized by
keeping a firm hold; determined

You must often be tenacious when
you learn vocabulary; don't give up
even when you find it useless.

99.
tenet
n.

any opinion, principle, doctrine,
dogma, etc., esp. one held as true by
members of a profession, group, or
movement

The most important tenet I live by is
"carpe diem"; I believe that every day
should be lived to the fullest.

100.
terminate
v.

to bring to an end, discontinue the
services of

The contract noted that either side
could terminate its provisions with a
30 day notice.

A. Fill in the appropriate words using the clues below.

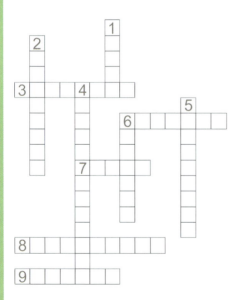

across:

3) n. reckless boldness; rashness
6) n. excess; an excessive amount
7) adj. smoothly agreeable or polite;
agreeably or blandly urbane
8) adj. uncultured in thought and manner
9) adj. having a sharp or bitter smell or
taste; to the point; penetrating

down:

1) adj. understood
2) adj. being inactive or quiet
4) adj. directed to the past; contemplative
of past situations, events
5) n. a severe reproof or rebuke, esp. a
formal one by a person in authority; (v.) to
reprove or rebuke severely
6) adj. able to pay all just debts; (n.) a
substance that dissolves another to form a
solution

B. Match the words on the left with their appropriate definitions on the right.

A. prudence _____ 1. adj. holding fast; characterized by keeping a firm hold; determined

B. rampant _____ 2. adj. inclined to silence; reserved in speech; reluctant to join in conversation

C. ravenous _____ 3. adj. being more than is sufficient or required; excessive

D. recalcitrant _____ 4. adj. resisting authority or control; not obedient or compliant

E. relegate _____ 5. adj. growing or occurring without restraint

F. render _____ 6. adj. calm, peaceful, or tranquil

G. repudiate _____ 7. adj. extremely hungry; famished

H. revere _____ 8. adj. characterized by or requiring a sitting posture

I. sanguine _____ 9. adj. inactive, sluggish, or dull

J. sedentary _____ 10. adj. expressed in few words; concise; terse

K. serene _____ 11. n. careful management; economy

L. sober _____ 12. adj. cheerfully optimistic, hopeful, or confident

M. somnolent _____ 13. adj. seemingly indifferent to or unaffected by pleasure or pain; impassive

N. stagnant _____ 14. v. to reject as having no authority or binding force

O. stoic _____ 15. v. to regard with respect tinged with awe

P. succinct _____ 16. adj. temperate, more realistic

Q. superfluous _____ 17. v. to send or consign to an inferior position, place or condition

R. sycophant _____ 18. adj. sleepy

S. taciturn _____ 19. n. a self-seeking, servile flatterer; fawning parasite

T. tenacious _____ 20. v. to cause to be or become; make

300pts

100pts

Week 10

terse

transfix

"The reward of a thing well done
is to have done it."
- Ralph Waldo Emerson

adj.

verb

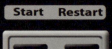
Start   Restart

1.

terse
adj.

neatly or effectively concise; brief as language

She comes across as rather terse, not saying much, but leaving one with the distinct impression that she was not happy.

2.

threshold
n.

the point of beginning; the outset

We were on the threshold of a major breakthrough when we noticed a critical error we had committed in our calculations.

3.

thwart
v.

to prevent the occurrence, realization, or attainment of

Mario thwarted all the fire-breathing monsters that tried to block his way and thereby won the game.

4.

tightfisted
adj.

stingy; tight

Ed was tightfisted with his money, arguing with the clerk at the 99 Cent Store that it was overcharging for some of the merchandise.

5.

timely
adj.

occurring at a suitable time; seasonable; well-timed

Please complete your work in a timely manner so that we can move on to our next exercise.

6.

timorous
adj.

lacking courage

The timorous young boy was so shy and afraid that his parents had to nudge him towards the famous artist to get an autograph.

7.

tinge
n.

a faint trace of color

We painted the wall mauve with a tinge of gray to tone the color down a bit.

8.

tirade
n.

long and angry violent speech

When the boss heard of her indiscretion and betrayal, he launched a scathing tirade against her in front of everyone.

WEEK 1
WEEK 2
WEEK 3
WEEK 4
WEEK 5
WEEK 6
WEEK 7
WEEK 8
WEEK 9
WEEK 10

REGULAR

9.

torpor

n.

apathy; lack of energy

The jungle's humidity put Frank into a state of torpor from which he could barely rouse himself.

10.

torrid

adj.

excessively hot; passionate

The torrid affair between the socialite and shipping heir was dragged out for weeks in the tabloids.

11.

tortuous

adj.

abounding in irregular bends or turns

The tortuous road up the mountains made me dizzy and slightly nauseous.

12.

torturous

adj.

marked by extreme suffering

As she drove past the asylum gates, Rita could hear the torturous cries of the patients within.

13.

tout

v.

to solicit customers, votes, or patronage; to promote or praise energetically; publicize

The late night infomercial touted the merits of having a razor that was eternally sharp, but all who were watching were justifiably skeptical.

14.

toxic

adj.

poisonous

The toxic waste dump wreaked havoc on the nearby community whose residents were becoming ill from the contamination.

15.

tractable

adj.

easily led or controlled

Farmers like a more tractable horse to help plow their fields.

16.

trajectory

n.

the path made by a projectile moving under given forces

The crowd held its breath as it watched the graceful trajectory of the football hurtling through the air.

17.

tranquil   adj.

calm

George sought a tranquil country place in which to finish his novel.

18.

transcript   n.

a copy made directly from an original

Transcripts of this program can be ordered for a small fee.

19.

transfiguration   n.

a marked change in form or appearance

Betty's transfiguration from a pale and frail little girl into a bright and blooming adolescent was astounding.

20.

transfix   v.

to render motionless, as with terror, amazement, or awe

The hikers were transfixed by the view of the beautiful valleys surrounding them.

21.

transfusion   n.

the act of pouring from one vessel to another

The injured policeman received a blood transfusion at the hospital after he nearly bled to death at the scene of the accident.

22.

transgress   v.

to break a law

The man feared going back to jail after he had transgressed the requirements of his parole.

23.

transience   n.

brevity of duration

She began to understand the transience of her fluctuating moods.

24.

translucent   adj.

allowing the passage of light

The waters along the shore were translucent, offering a vivid display of their brightly colored inhabitants.

WEEK 1
WEEK 2
WEEK 3
WEEK 4
WEEK 5
WEEK 6
WEEK 7
WEEK 8
WEEK 9
WEEK 10

REGULAR

25.

transmute

v.

to change in nature, substance, or form

Count Dracula's remarkable powers allowed him to transmute from a man into a vampire bat.

26.

travail

n.

hard or agonizing labor

The travails of life are inevitable; the only thing you can do in the face of them is change your attitude.

27.

travesty

n.

a grotesque imitation; mockery

The non-guilty verdict was considered to be such a travesty of justice that citizens took to the streets in protest.

28.

treacherous

adj.

characterized by faithlessness or readiness to betray trust; traitorous; deceptive, untrustworthy, or unreliable

No one could trust the blacksmith anymore when it was discovered that he was part of a treacherous scheme to steal the king's money.

29.

trepidation

n.

tremulous fear, alarm, or agitation

With trepidation, the squire crept closer to the dragon's den, fearing the fierce power of its fiery breath.

30.

trite

adj.

made commonplace by frequent repetition

A serious and studious person will not easily tolerate the trite conversations of average people.

31.

truculent

adj.

aggressive and bad-tempered; expressing bitter opposition; violent and fierce

As we approached the border, the truculent soldiers gave us a steely-eyed death stare.

32.

trudge

v.

to walk, esp. laboriously or wearily

The family trudged through the deepening snow seeking to find shelter from the blizzard.

33.

truncate
v.

to shorten by cutting off a part; cut short

On the back of the one dollar bill is a picture of a truncated pyramid, its top not completed and replaced by the all-seeing eye.

34.

tumult
n.

the din and commotion of a great crowd

The tumult of the party upstairs prevented us from sleeping all night.

35.

turbulent
adj.

being in a state of agitation or tumult; disturbed

Most of the shaking that one feels on an aircraft comes from mild, but turbulent, air that lifts the plane.

36.

unbecoming
adj.

unsuited to the wearer, place, or surroundings

The man, wearing a dirty T-shirt and jeans, was an unbecoming sight to some of the more sophisticated members of the audience.

37.

unbridled
adj.

being without restraint

The unbridled horse was difficult to control after the deafening gunshot.

38.

unconscionable
adj.

ridiculously or unjustly excessive

The spoiled hotel heiress' lawyer called her 45-day prison sentence unconscionable and undeserved.

39.

uncouth
adj.

awkward, clumsy, or unmannerly

I can't stand Frankie's uncouth behavior; he screams at anyone who serves him, demanding that the server meet his every need.

40.

underhanded
adj.

sneaky and deceptive

Since the banker knew he would never win using legitimate means, he used underhanded methods to rig the election.

WEEK 1
WEEK 2
WEEK 3
WEEK 4
WEEK 5
WEEK 6
WEEK 7
WEEK 8
WEEK 9
WEEK 10
REGULAR

41.
underling   n.
a subordinate

The underlings at the law firm often work sixty-hour work weeks while the partners lounge about in the coffee shop downstairs.

42.
underpinning   n.
a support or foundation

The underpinning of success in any field is determination.

43.
undulate   v.
to move like a wave or in waves

Rita was moved to see the flag of her native country as it undulated in the breeze.

44.
unilateral   adj.
of, involving, or affecting only one side

The Secretary of State warned against the unilateral approach to foreign policy that the President's administration wanted to take.

45.
unkempt   adj.
not properly maintained; disorderly or untidy; sloppy

The law school student looked unkempt with his disheveled clothing and clearly uncombed hair.

46.
unlettered   adj.
not adept at reading or writing

The unlettered members of our community would benefit from literacy training.

47.
unmalleable   adj.
difficult or impossible to shape or work

I can't work with that metal since it is unmalleable even in the most extreme heat and pressure.

48.
unspeakable   adj.
beyond description; inexpressibly bad or evil

Six million Jews endured unspeakable horrors in German concentration camps.

49.
untenable
adj.

being such that defense or maintenance is impossible

Your argument is untenable; it is unlikely that you will win your case in court.

50.
untimely
adj.

occurring before an expected time; occurring at an inappropriate or inopportune time

The untimely death of the family's two heirs left the estate in disarray.

51.
urbane
adj.

having the polish regarded as characteristic of sophisticated social life in major cities

Franklin was unlike his sister, more urbane and sophisticated than crude and unsociable.

52.
utility
n.

fitness for some desirable practical purpose

The tool's utility cannot be overstated; it features three blades, three screwdrivers, and a bottle opener.

53.
utter
v.

to articulate, pronounce, or speak

"If you utter one word of my secret to anyone else," said Justine, "I'll hate you forever!"

54.
vacant
adj.

having no occupant; unoccupied

The apartment was vacant after the family had moved.

55.
vacate
v.

to leave; to cease to occupy

We were ordered to vacate the premises by next month for failure to pay rent.

56.
vaccinate
v.

to inoculate with vaccine in order to produce immunity to disease

I was vaccinated for measles before I was allowed to attend public school.

WEEK 1
WEEK 2
WEEK 3
WEEK 4
WEEK 5
WEEK 6
WEEK 7
WEEK 8
WEEK 9
WEEK 10

REGULAR

57.

vacillate

v.

to waver

Mel's temper vacillated wildly between rage and serenity.

58.

vagabond

n.

a wanderer, esp. one with no permanent home

The life of a hobo or vagabond is sometimes romanticized; people don't realize how hard it is to be homeless.

59.

valiant

adj.

boldly courageous; brave; stout-hearted

Sir Galahad led the valiant knights in the war against the invading Huns.

60.

valorous

adj.

courageous

The three valorous soldiers who stayed on the battlefield when everyone else retreated were awarded Medals of Honor for their brave efforts.

61.

vapid

adj.

dull and uninteresting; lacking liveliness

Jacob refused to listen to any more of the girls' vapid conversation.

62.

variance

n.

change

The detective kept questioning us over and over to check if he could find variances in our stories.

63.

veil

v.

to conceal or disguise

Juliet could no longer veil her longing for Romeo.

64.

venerable

adj.

worthy of great respect and reverence, esp. because of age or wisdom

The venerable judge Felix Frankfurter spoke at the opening of the new department.

65.

venerate

v.

to cherish reverentially

Older men and women need to be venerated for their wisdom and the years in which they served their families and communities.

66.

veracity

n.

truthfulness

The veracity of the statements in court went unchallenged; the witness's tears and evident remorse spoke for themselves.

67.

verbose

adj.

characterized by the use of many or too many words; wordy

The large number of verbose speakers for the Oscars caused the event to be five hours long.

68.

verity

n.

truth

I challenge the verity of your claim that you met Elvis yesterday.

69.

vestige

n.

a visible trace, mark, or impression, of something absent, lost, or gone

Not a vestige of the summer village was left after the tribe dismantled their huts and headed for winter camp.

70.

vie

v.

to contend

The two suitors vied for Violetta's romantic attentions.

71.

vigilant

adj.

being on the alert to discover and ward off danger or insure safety

The vigilant sailor, lost out at sea for weeks, finally spotted dry land after squinting out into the dark during the huge storm.

72.

vilify

v.

to speak ill of; defame; slander

Rick would vilify anyone who didn't support the Dodgers or the Lakers.

WEEK 1
WEEK 2
WEEK 3
WEEK 4
WEEK 5
WEEK 6
WEEK 7
WEEK 8
WEEK 9
WEEK 10

REGULAR

73.

vindictive

adj.

revengeful

A vindictive person will seek occasions for revenge.

74.

virtuoso

n.

a master in the technique of some particular fine art

The virtuoso played scales effortlessly and captivated his audience with his technical ease and lyrical melodies.

75.

virulent

adj.

exceedingly noxious or harmful

The doctor had to amputate his leg after a virulent insect bite.

76.

visage

n.

the face, countenance, or look of a person

The totem pole was topped with a mysterious visage resembling Santa Claus.

77.

voluminous

adj.

large and bulky

The bride's voluminous gown brushed against the pews as she walked down the church aisle.

78.

voracious

adj.

eating with greediness or in very large quantities.

The reptiles on the island are known for their voracious appetites.

79.

vulgarity

n.

lack of refinement in conduct or speech

After several years of etiquette training, Beth was able to purge herself of her former vulgarity.

80.

wanting

adj.

to be without; lack

The young intern did her work sloppily and carelessly, leading her boss to comment that her work was wanting at best.

81.

warrant
n.

authorization, as given by a superior;
justification for an action or a belief

The judge determined that while the
evidence was inconclusive, it certainly
warranted a closer look by the state.

82.

wary
adj.

watchful; being on one's guard
against danger

I would be wary about getting closer
than a few hundred feet to that herd of
buffalo.

83.

wayward
adj.

given or marked by willful deviation
from the norm

The wayward teenager was sent to a
correctional facility by his parents in
hopes that he'd be rid of his vices.

84.

wheedle
v.

to endeavor to influence (a person)
by smooth, flattering, or beguiling
words or acts

She wheedled her husband into
writing letters to their three sons in
college.

85.

whim
n.

a sudden capricious idea or fancy

He is usually afraid of the dark but last
night he had a sudden whim to take a
midnight walk.

86.

wholesome
adj.

conducive to moral or general
well-being; beneficial

We all want to live wholesome and
safe lives, free from moral chaos and
crime.

87.

wile
n.

an act or a means of cunning
deception

The young woman used her female
wiles to attract the attention of the
wealthy, old businessman.

88.

winsome
adj.

charming, often in a childlike way

His winsome expression made
everyone like him.

WEEK 1
WEEK 2
WEEK 3
WEEK 4
WEEK 5
WEEK 6
WEEK 7
WEEK 8
WEEK 9
WEEK 10

REGULAR

89.

wit   n.

keen perception; the ability to use this intelligence to create humor

Shakespeare's wit takes some examining, but the reader who can understand his humor will be rewarded with clearer understanding of his plays.

90.

witticism   n.

a witty, brilliant, or original saying or sentiment

Ben Franklin was well known for his witticisms, which is not surprising because he clearly had a mastery of both words and ideas.

91.

wittingly   adv.

with knowledge and by design

The jury determined that the defendant wittingly murdered the victim rather than accidentally killing him as the defendant's lawyer had tried to argue.

92.

wooden   adj.

stiff or unnatural; without spirit

Why did the Democratic party choose such a wooden candidate to run for president?

93.

worldly   adj.

experienced; knowing; sophisticated

When in the city, she often looked for sophisticated restaurants and clubs, where the most worldly people could be found.

94.

wrangle   v.

to maintain by noisy argument or dispute

My brothers wrangled with each other noisily in the parking lot, creating an embarrassing spectacle.

95.

wreak   v.

to inflict, as a revenge or punishment

Their exuberant grandson ran around the house, wreaking havoc like a tiny tornado.

96.

writhe   v.

to twist the body, face, or limbs as in pain or distress

The earthworms writhed when exposed to the bright light.

97.

wry

adj.

dryly humorous, often with a touch of irony

Grandpa gave us a wry wink when he showed us he was hiding Grandma's lost diamond earring in his pocket.

98.

yield

v.

submitting to another; to surrender

Because the driver did not yield to the oncoming traffic, he caused a ten-car pileup.

99.

yore

n.

time past

Sharon had no interest in modern buildings; she was more enamored with the castles of yore.

100.

zenith

n.

a highest point or state; culmination

People kept wondering when Tiger Woods would hit the zenith of his career.

A. Fill in the appropriate words using the clues below.

across:

2) v. to speak ill of; defame; slander
4) n. a visible trace, mark, or impression, of something absent, lost, or gone
5) n. a highest point or state; culmination
7) v. to break a law
8) v. to move like a wave or in waves

down:

1) v. to shorten by cutting off a part; cut short
2) n. truthfulness
3) adj. lacking courage
4) adj. revengeful
6) n. hard or agonizing labor

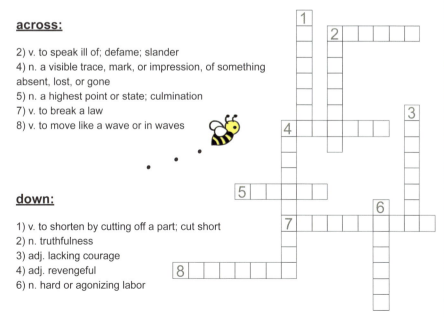

WEEK 1
WEEK 2
WEEK 3
WEEK 4
WEEK 5
WEEK 6
WEEK 7
WEEK 8
WEEK 9
WEEK 10

REGULAR

B. Match the words on the left with their appropriate definitions on the right.

A. terse   _____   1. v. to twist the body, face, or limbs as in pain or distress

B. tirade   _____   2. adj. made commonplace by frequent repetition

C. tractable   _____   3. adj. easily led or controlled

D. transience   _____   4. n. the face, countenance, or look of a person

E. trite   _____   5. adj. having the polish regarded as characteristic of sophisticated social life in major cities

F. truculent   _____   6. adj. awkward, clumsy, or unmannerly

G. turbulent   _____   7. adj. not properly maintained; disorderly or untidy; sloppy

H. uncouth   _____   8. adj. having no contents; empty; void; having no occupant; unoccupied

I. unkempt   _____   9. adj. eating with greediness or in very large quantities

J. urbane   _____ 10. n. long and angry violent speech

K. vacant   _____ 11. adj. characterized by the use of many or too many words; wordy

L. vapid   _____ 12. n. authorization, as given by a superior; justification for an action or belief

M. verbose   _____ 13. adj. experienced; knowing; sophisticated

N. vigilant   _____ 14. n. a master in the technique of some particular fine art

O. virtuoso   _____ 15. adj. being on the alert to discover and ward off danger or insure safety

P. visage   _____ 16. adj. dull and uninteresting; lacking liveliness

Q. voracious   _____ 17. adj. being in a state of agitation or tumult; disturbed

R. warrant   _____ 18. adj. neatly or effectively concise; brief as language

S. worldly   _____ 19. adj. aggressive and bad-tempered; expressing bitter opposition; violent and fierce

T. writhe   _____ 20. n. brevity of duration

Stage 1 Complete!
GOAL!!
atone
blazon
decrepit
enrapture
frolicsome
indomitable
misconstrue
preoccupation
retrospective
unconscionable
Start
Restart
A
B

Congratulations on reaching the next level of your SAT prep! Start here to further increase your vocabulary skills!

Press START for the
Advanced Level

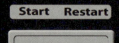
Start   Restart

A

B

100pts

300pts

Week 1

aver

affront

"The will to persevere is often the difference between failure and success."
- David Sarnoff

verb

noun

1.

abase

v.

to lower in position, esteem, or rank; degrade

Tom would constantly abase others publicly, making them feel like less than what they were worth.

2.

aberration

n.

deviation from a right, customary, or prescribed course

Polar bears' eating their own young is an aberration in their normal behavior.

3.

abject

adj.

utterly hopeless, miserable, humiliating, or wretched

Parts of sub-Saharan Africa has suffered generations of abject poverty, each person earning only about $100 a year.

4.

abjure

v.

to recant, renounce, repudiate under oath

After his research, he had to abjure his former position and dismiss the theory that one could ever time travel.

5.

abnegate

v.

to renounce or give up a right or privilege

Students who wished to experience Victorian times abnegated the luxury of computers for a month.

6.

abominable

adj.

deserving hatred; horrible; unpleasant or disagreeable

The girls found everyone else in class to have an abominable taste in clothing.

7.

aboriginal

adj.

primitive; unsophisticated

The museum of Sydney, Australia has some of the finest pottery made by aboriginal peoples who inhabited the continent 1000 years ago.

8.

abrogate

v.

to abolish, repeal

The mayor abrogated the previous policies and instituted entirely new ones.

9.

abscond
v.

to depart in a sudden and secret manner, esp. to avoid capture and legal prosecution

After he stole all the money, the bank manager absconded by fleeing to Cancun.

10.

abstemious
adj.

sparing or moderate in eating and drinking; temperate diet

Ever since he became wealthy and began to live in luxury and indulgence, there was nothing abstemious about him.

11.

abut
v.

to be adjacent; touch or join at the edge or border

That house will be constructed in such a way that it will abut the house next door.

12.

acme
n.

the highest point; summit; peak

To reach the acme of his career, Ned had to show that he could sell a thousand iPods in one month.

13.

adjudicate
v.

to settle a dispute; to pronounce or decree by judicial sentence

The principal adjudicated the quarrel between the two students.

14.

adulterate
n.

to make a substance impure by adding bad or unnecessary ingredients

The batch of chocolate syrup was adulterated when someone accidentally added industrial cleanser to the mixture.

15.

affront
n.

an open insult or indignity

Though he meant well, Steve came across harshly; his speech was deemed an affront to the president of the club.

16.

aggrandize
v.

to make greater or to cause to appear greater

The new biography aggrandizes his role in the revolution.

WEEK 1
WEEK 2
WEEK 3
WEEK 4
WEEK 5
WEEK 6
WEEK 7
WEEK 8
WEEK 9
WEEK 10

ADVANCED

17.

alacrity n.

cheerful readiness, promptness, or willingness; speed

Because he wanted to go to the high school dance later that night, Willis did his chores with alacrity.

18.

allay v.

to put (fear, doubt, suspicion, anger, etc.) to rest; calm; quiet

His mom allayed Jeff's fears of driving by taking him out to a country road and allowing him to drive in a less populated area.

19.

ameliorate v.

to make or become better, more bearable, or more satisfactory

The pain in her leg was ameliorated once she was sedated.

20.

amity n.

friendship; peaceful relations

Russia believed that the amity it showed to others was vital in maintaining its strong presence in the world.

21.

amorphous adj.

lacking definite form; having no specific shape; formless

An amoeba is a microscopic animal that is amorphous in shape, shifting its form depending on its liquid environment.

22.

anachronistic adj.

pertaining to or containing something or someone that is not in its correct historical or chronological time, esp. a thing or person that belongs to an earlier time

Writing a history paper involving dinosaurs and Martin Luther King, Jr. roaming the earth at the same time seems a bit anachronistic.

23.

ancillary n.

of secondary or subordinate importance, yet still helpful

In the hospital, she was hired as an ancillary surgeon, filling in when the administration needed her for emergencies.

24.

anesthetic adj.

pertaining to or producing loss of sensation

When Eva had a root canal, the dentist gave her an anesthetic drug to ease the pain.

25.

anomalous   adj.

unusual in nature, deviating from the norm

Experiencing a visit from some form of extraterrestrial life would be an anomalous event.

26.

apex   n.

the tip, point, or vertex; summit

Baseball slugger Willie Mays reached the apex of his career when he hit his 600th career home run in 1968.

27.

apogee   n.

the highest or most distant point from the Earth

The spacecraft reached the apogee of its orbit, traveling 15,000 miles above the Earth's surface.

28.

apostasy   n.

a total departure from one's faith or religion

Church officials removed the priest from his duties since he was judged guilty of apostasy in denying the existence of God.

29.

apprise   v.

to inform, give notice to

To make the best decision, the President needs to be fully apprised of the situation.

30.

ascertain   v.

learn with definity or certainty

From the evidence found in the paleontological dig, the scientists were able to ascertain the approximate time of the dinosaur's death.

31.

ascribe   v.

to credit or assign, as to a cause or source; attribute

They ascribed honor and glory to the military regiment that had marched into the enemy's territory and taken out the opposing forces with hardly any loss of life.

32.

asinine   adj.

foolish, unintelligent, or silly; stupid

Thinking that you will drive around the world in less than two months is one of the most asinine ideas you have ever come up with.

WEEK 1
WEEK 2
WEEK 3
WEEK 4
WEEK 5
WEEK 6
WEEK 7
WEEK 8
WEEK 9
WEEK 10

ADVANCED

33.

attest

v.

to bear witness to; certify; declare to be correct, true, or genuine; declare the truth of, in word or writing, esp. affirm in an official capacity

I can attest to where the defendant was during the time of the burglary.

34.

augur

v.

to interpret omens for guidance

The ancient priest thought the strange star he had observed augured doom for the emperor.

35.

auxiliary

adj.

additional; supplementary; reserve; (n.) a person or thing that gives aid of any kind; helper

He was an auxiliary member of the fire department, called upon when all full members were either away or on duty.

36.

avaricious

adj.

greedy; covetous

The young girl with a platinum credit card walked along Rodeo Drive, eyeing all the expensive clothes in an avaricious manner.

37.

aver

v.

to assert or affirm with confidence; declare in a positive or peremptory manner

The President averred that the war in Iraq would last longer than expected.

38.

avidity

n.

eagerness; greediness

Wall Street is often filled with investors and speculators motivated by the lowest avidity known to man.

39.

awry

adv.

away from the expected direction; with a turn or twist to one side

Our plans for a perfect summer vacation went awry when our father enrolled us in summer school.

40.

bequeath

v.

to dispose of (personal property, esp. money) by last will

The grandmother bequeathed the family heirlooms to her eldest granddaughter, who she believed would take the best care of them.

41.

blasé   adj.

indifferent to or bored with life; unimpressed, as or as if from an excess of worldly pleasures

Their blasé attitude contributed to a feeling of apathy among all the workers in that department.

42.

brazen   adj.

shameless or impudent

Once having been a reckless, brazen frontiersman, Jack is now a humble and docile grandfather of ten.

43.

bulwark   n.

anything that gives security or defense

The wall constructed on the outskirts of the city served as a bulwark against future floods.

44.

burgeon   v.

grow quickly and expansively

The flowers began to burgeon in the springtime, blooming in beautiful pinks, reds, and whites.

45.

burnish   v.

to make brilliant or shining; to polish

The maid burnished the silverware so much that it reflected her image like a mirror.

46.

cache   n.

place in which valuables are stored

The thief put the stolen jewels in a cache behind a family picture hanging over the fireplace.

47.

cadence   n.

rhythmical or measured flow or movement of words

The music progressed at a steady cadence which sped up toward the finale.

48.

callow   adj.

without experience of the world; immature

Having never held a job before, the callow young engineer had no idea how to deal with people in the workplace.

WEEK 1
WEEK 2
WEEK 3
WEEK 4
WEEK 5
WEEK 6
WEEK 7
WEEK 8
WEEK 9
WEEK 10

ADVANCED

49.

canon   n.

an established principle; a law or
group of laws

The canons of polite society dictate
that all civilized people should chew
with their mouths closed.

50.

capacious   adj.

roomy

We bought a capacious new house
that was ten times the size of the tiny
one-bedroom apartment.

A. Fill in the appropriate words using the clues below.

across:

1) adj. unusual in nature; deviating from
the norm
3) v. to inform, give notice to
6) n. to make a substance impure by
adding bad or unnecessary ingredients
8) v. to be adjacent; touch or join at the
edge
9) adj. deserving hatred; horrible;
unpleasant or disagreeable

down:

2) v. to assert or affirm with confidence;
declare in a positive or peremptory manner
3) eagerness; greediness
4) v. to make greater or to cause to appear
greater
5) adj. indifferent to or bored with life;
unimpressed, as or as if from an excess of
worldly pleasures
7) n. anything that gives security or defense

B. Match the words on the left with their appropriate definitions on the right.

A. abase _____ 1. v. grow quickly and expansively

B. aberration _____ 2. adv. with a turn or twist to one side; askew

C. abject _____ 3. v. to make or become better, more bearable, or more satisfactory

D. abnegate _____ 4. n. the tip, point, or vertex; summit

E. abscond _____ 5. adj. lacking definite form; having no specific shape; formless

F. adjudicate _____ 6. v. learn with definiteness or certainty

G. affront _____ 7. adj. additional; supplementary; reserve; (n.) a person or thing that gives aid of any kind; helper

H. alacrity _____ 8. n. cheerful readiness, promptness, or willingness; speed

I. ameliorate _____ 9. n. deviation from a right, customary, or prescribed course

J. amorphous _____10. v. to depart in a sudden and secret manner, esp. to avoid capture and legal prosecution

K. apex _____11. v. to bear witness to; certify; declare to be correct, true, or genuine

L. ascertain _____12. adj. without experience of the world; immature

M. ascribe _____13. v. to renounce or give up a right or privilege

N. attest _____14. v. to credit or assign, as to a cause or source; attribute

O. auxiliary _____15. adj. shameless or impudent

P. avaricious _____16. v. to lower in position, esteem, or rank; degrade

Q. awry _____17. n. an open insult or indignity

R. brazen _____18. v. to settle a dispute; to pronounce or decree by judicial sentence

S. burgeon _____19. adj. utterly hopeless, miserable, humiliating, or wretched

T. callow _____20. adj. greedy; covetous

WEEK 1
WEEK 2
WEEK 3
WEEK 4
WEEK 5
WEEK 6
WEEK 7
WEEK 8
WEEK 9
WEEK 10

ADVANCED

300pts

100pts

Week 2

cull

cognate

 **"Persistence is the twin sister of excellence.
One is a matter of quality;
the other, a matter of time."
- Marabel Morgan**

 verb

adj.

Start   Restart

 A

B

1.

capitulate

v.

to surrender

When the army general realized that the battle could not be won, he decided to capitulate.

2.

captious

adj.

faultfinding; hypercritical

The countess was a naturally captious woman who managed to find fault with every little task and had difficulty praising people.

3.

carouse

v.

to engage in a drunken revel

The fraternity boys knew they were in trouble when they caroused well into the next day, mere hours before their final examination for History 101.

4.

carp

v.

nag; irritably and constantly complain

Jack's wife was constantly carping about her friends at the country club; Jack merely pretended to listen to her complaining.

5.

caste

n.

the class and rank or position of somebody in a society, based on birth, occupation,etc.

The country has an unfair system: the lighter your skin, the higher your caste.

6.

castigate

v.

to criticize or reprimand severely

The teacher castigated the entire class for scoring no higher than a "C" on the vocabulary test.

7.

cataclysm

n.

violent upheaval that causes great destruction or brings about fundamental change

The 1994 Northridge Earthquake was a great cataclysm for Southern California.

8.

cession

n.

surrender, as of possessions or rights

Japan's cession of the island of Formosa to the Chinese occurred in 1895.

WEEK 1
WEEK 2
WEEK 3
WEEK 4
WEEK 5
WEEK 6
WEEK 7
WEEK 8
WEEK 9
WEEK 10

ADVANCED

9.
chivalry   n.

courteous behavior, esp. by men toward women; the qualities idealized by medieval knights, such as honor, bravery, and gallantry

Despite many complaints from women, chivalry is not dead; some men still open doors and pull out chairs for women.

10.
choleric   adj.

easily provoked to anger

I have memories of my choleric father blowing words out of proportion and picking fights at restaurants for no apparent reason.

11.
churlish   adj.

rude, unsociable

The teacher usually removed him from the room for his churlish behavior, which distracted other students from learning.

12.
circumlocution   n.

a roundabout or indirect way of asking; the use of more words than necessary to express an idea

Norm's memos were known for having too much circumlocution; anyone who read them was puzzled about his intentions.

13.
clangor   n.

clanking or a ringing, as of arms, chains, or bells; clamor

The clangor of the church bells on Sunday morning drowned out the songs of the birds.

14.
clone   n.

a cell, cell product, or organism that is genetically identical to the unit or individual from which it was derived

He made clones of his pet rabbit and then sold them as gifts to children for Easter.

15.
cloying   adj.

unnaturally sweet; excessively sentimental

The cloying apple pie must have been made with the whole bag of sugar!

16.
coalescence   n.

the act or process of coming together so as to form one body, combination, or product

The coalescence of the tiny cloud droplets produced much larger drops of water.

17.

cognate   adj.

of the same or similar nature

Some scholars argue that Chinese and Japanese are cognate languages.

18.

colloquial   adj.

related to informal language

We were instructed to avoid using colloquial terms in our essays.

19.

commiserate   v.

share feelings with, particularly those of sadness or disappointment

It's nice to have good friends whom you can tell your problems to and commiserate with.

20.

complaisant   adj.

agreeable

Generally a complaisant young lady, she surprised us with her vehement opposition to our proposition.

21.

compunction   n.

remorseful feeling

Her compunction was obviously genuine, as the young girl wept when she confessed that she had made a terrible mistake.

22.

conduce   v.

to bring about a desired result

I knew that introducing my two friends would conduce to a mutual happiness.

23.

conflagration   n.

a great fire, as of many buildings, a forest, or the like

The great earthquake in San Francisco at the turn of the century was followed by an equally great conflagration that left the city in ashes.

24.

congenital   adj.

of or pertaining to a condition present at birth, whether inherited or caused by the environment

Because the condition Denise had was a congenital one, no change in her diet or exercise regimen could prevent her from suffering from it.

WEEK 1
WEEK 2
WEEK 3
WEEK 4
WEEK 5
WEEK 6
WEEK 7
WEEK 8
WEEK 9
WEEK 10
ADVANCED

25.

conjugate   adj.

joined together in pairs

The crayons came in conjugate pairs, but we had to break several of them apart whenever we each wanted one of the colors.

26.

connote   v.

to mean; signify; to suggest or imply in addition to literal meaning

Her cold stare connoted to us that we were not welcome in her house.

27.

consign   v.

to entrust

You have no choice but to consign your baggage to the airline, and it is not guaranteed to arrive safely at your destination.

28

consort   n.

a companion or associate

My consort and I will be happy to attend the party celebrating the success of your new company.

29.

consulate   n.

the place in which a consul transacts official business

While on vacation in China, my friends and I had to visit the American consulate to ask about passport issues.

30.

consummate   v.

to bring to completion

They consummated the business talks by signing a binding agreement.

31.

contiguous   adj.

touching or joining at the edge or boundary

There are 48 contiguous states in the United States, since neither Alaska nor Hawaii borders any other state.

32.

continence   n.

self-restraint with respect to desires, appetites, and passion

I exhibited surprising continence at the buffet; ordinarily, I would have eaten everything in sight, but today I had just one plate of food.

33.

contingency   n.

possibility of happening

Our plan must allow for certain contingencies, so that we won't be caught off guard.

34.

contravene   v.

to prevent or obstruct the operation of

The defense lawyer's continued attempts to contravene the line of questioning by the district attorney soon incurred the wrath of the judge.

35.

contrivance   n.

something that is devised or adapted for or to a special purpose; a deceitful method or plan; an artificial and obviously false arrangement

Our scientists' contrivance of the new machines suited their needs perfectly and made their jobs much easier.

36.

coquettish   adj.

acting in a flirtatious manner

With a coquettish smile, the young girl winked at the boy who had been staring at her.

37.

cornucopia   n.

a horn overflowing with fruit and grains, symbolizing prosperity; any abundance

After three hours, the committee came up with a virtual cornucopia of ideas on how to better manage traffic congestion.

38.

corollary   n.

a proposition following so obviously from another that it requires little demonstration

The Roosevelt Corollary was simply a logical consequence of the preexisting Monroe Doctrine.

39.

corrigible   adj.

capable of reformation

The judge, thinking that the juvenile was corrigible, decided to sentence him to counseling rather than jail time.

40.

cosmopolitan   adj.

free from local, provincial, or national ideas, prejudices, or attachments; at home all over the world.; (n.) citizen of the world

Mumbai has, over the past twenty years, turned into India's most cosmopolitan city, drawing visitors and new residents from around the world.

WEEK 1
WEEK 2
WEEK 3
WEEK 4
WEEK 5
WEEK 6
WEEK 7
WEEK 8
WEEK 9
WEEK 10

ADVANCED

41.
coterie n.
a group of people who associate closely

Cherry walked in with her coterie, seven other snobbish young women who expected to make the finals of the beauty pageant.

42.
coy adj.
artfully or affectedly shy or reserved; slyly hesitant; coquettish

She was coy with Frederick because she wanted him to pursue her, but she did not want to appear too easily available for him.

43.
craven adj.
cowardly; contemptibly timid; pusillanimous; (n.) a coward

He has an appearance of a tough man but he is actually a craven fellow who turns and runs whenever a conflict arises.

44.
crony n.
a close friend or companion; chum

The mayor hired his old crony from high school to become police commissioner.

45.
crucible n.
a severe test or trial

The crucible of the witches was nothing more than a conspiracy to get rid of free-thinking women.

46.
cull v.
to choose; select; pick; (n.) act of culling

The hungry wolves culled the sick members from the herd of sheep and cornered them.

47.
cupidity n.
excessive desire; greed

Ironically, the businessman's cupidity grew as he got richer; the more money he had, the more money he wanted.

48.
curmudgeon n.
an irritable, bad-tempered individual

Our neighbor is such a curmudgeon that he frowned derisively when we showed him pictures of our newborn kittens.

49.

debonair   adj.

courteous, gracious, and having a
sophisticated charm

In his tuxedo and top hat, he pranced
into the ballroom, the most debonair
dancer in the room.

50.

declamation   n.

a speech recited or intended for
recitation from memory in public

The most famous words in President's
Roosevelt's speech after the attack on
Pearl Harbor was his declamation,
"This day shall live in infamy."

A. Fill in the appropriate words using the clues below.

down:

1) n. an irritable, bad-tempered
individual
2) n. a companion or associate
3) adj. capable of reformation
4) n. surrender, as of possessions
or rights
6) v. to entrust

across:

2) v. to choose; select; pick
3) n. clanking or a ringing, as of
arms, chains, or bells; clamor
5) v. to bring about a desired result
6) to engage in a drunken revel
7) n. the act or process of coming
together so as to form one body,
combination, or product

WEEK 1
WEEK 2
WEEK 3
WEEK 4
WEEK 5
WEEK 6
WEEK 7
WEEK 8
WEEK 9
WEEK 10

ADVANCED

B. Match the words on the left with their appropriate definitions on the right.

A. capitulate _____ 1. adj. acting in a flirtatious manner

B. castigate _____ 2. adj. cowardly; contemptibly timid; pusillanimous; (n.) a coward; (v.) to make cowardly

C. circumlocution_____ 3. v. to mean; signify; to suggest or imply in addition to literal meaning

D. cloying _____ 4. adj. agreeable

E. commiserate _____ 5. n. a great fire, as of many buildings, a forest, or the like

F. complaisant _____ 6. v. share feelings with, particularly those of sadness or disappointment

G. compunction _____ 7. n. something that is devised or adapted for or to a special purpose; a deceitful method or plan

H. conflagration _____ 8. n. a group of people who associate closely

I. connote _____ 9. n. a possibility of happening

J. consummate _____ 10. adj. courteous, gracious, and having a sophisticated air

K. contingency _____ 11. v. to surrender

L. contrivance _____ 12. v. to choose; select; pick; (n.) act of culling

M. coquettish _____ 13. v. to bring to completion

N. corollary _____ 14. adj. free from local, provincial, or national ideas, prejudices, or attachments

O. cosmopolitan _____ 15. n. a roundabout or indirect way of asking; the use of more words than necessary to express an idea

P. coterie _____ 16. n. a proposition following so obviously from another that it requires little demonstration

Q. cull _____ 17. n. excessive desire; greed

R. craven _____ 18. adj. unnaturally sweet; excessively sentimental

S. cupidity _____ 19. v. to criticize or reprimand severely

T. debonair _____ 20. n. remorseful feeling

100pts

300pts

Week 3

dour

duress

"It's funny about life: if you refuse to
accept anything but the very best
you will very often get it."
- William Somerset Maugham

adj.

noun

Start   Restart

 A

 B

1.

deem   v.

to hold as an opinion; think

The wealthy businessman's wife deemed the clothing too cheap for her tastes and rejected it.

2.

deign   v.

to deem worthy of notice or account; to condescend

The President would not deign to meet with the mother of the slain soldier, since she had been so openly critical of his policies.

3.

demur   v.

to object to, often in a coy or flirtatious way

When asked to share his opinion, the public figure demurred and remained silent for fear of offending anybody.

4.

denote   v.

to be a mark or sign of; indicate

The term "Ms."--as opposed to "Miss" or "Mrs."--does not denote any marital status.

5.

denude   v.

to strip of covering, esp. foliage

After the invasion of caterpillars last summer, the trees were denuded of their leaves.

6.

deprecate   v.

to express disapproval of; to show contempt for, belittle

The manager constantly deprecates the efforts of others without ever examining his own ability.

7.

desultory   adj.

occurring in a random or haphazard way; disconnected; having no set plan; sloppy

The children were given to desultory fits of conversation which frustrated their math teacher greatly.

8.

diatribe   n.

a bitter, sharply abusive denunciation, attack, or criticism

The frustrated director subjected the entire film crew to a long diatribe against sloppiness.

9.

dichotomy n.

a division into two opposing parts

The dichotomy between Eastern and Western influences and customs could not be more apparent.

10.

dictum n.

an authoritative and formal pronouncement

The king's dictum was considered the law of the land.

11.

dilatory adj.

tending to cause delay

The dilatory soldier held up the entire platoon when he fell so far behind that others had to backtrack to look for him.

12.

dilettante n.

an amateur who engages in an activity without serious intentions and who pretends to have knowledge

Leon was merely a dilettante in the field of medieval art, so no one took him seriously when he tried to show how much he knew during the field trip to the museum.

13.

dirge n.

funeral song, strong expression of mourning

A dirge was played at the funeral to commemorate the man's life.

14.

disaffect v.

to cause to lose affection, sympathy or support

Mary was disaffected by the decisions of the current administration and decided that during the next election she would definitely vote for the other guy.

15.

discountenance v.

to look upon with disfavor

The king unwisely discountenanced his few loyal subjects only to find himself alone in a hostile court.

16.

disenfranchise v.

to deprive of any right, privilege, or power

For many years before the revolution, the poor were disenfranchised of the right to vote.

WEEK 1
WEEK 2
WEEK 3
WEEK 4
WEEK 5
WEEK 6
WEEK 7
WEEK 8
WEEK 9
WEEK 10

ADVANCED

17.

disingenuous adj.

lacking in frankness, candor, or sincerity; falsely or hypocritically ingenuous; insincere

Don't you find it a bit disingenuous to say you love her when she is not your only girlfriend?

18.

disparity n.

lack of similarity or equality; inequality; difference

The disparities in our salaries was evident; while she was buying diamond necklaces and BMWs, I was still in debt and barely scraping by.

19.

disputatious adj.

argumentative; contentious

The Congressmen spent the whole week arguing over the budget, but nothing got done in such a disputatious environment.

20.

dissentious adj.

disagreeing with the majority opinion; causing divisiveness

The dissentious party organized a huge parade in hopes of protecting the minority opinion and garnering support for their cause.

21.

dissertation n.

a long, formal thesis, especially one written to obtain a doctoral degree

Ph.D. students write a dissertation at the end of their studies to show mastery over a particular area of academic discipline.

22.

distend v.

to stretch out or expand in every direction

The balloon continued to distend; we were afraid it would pop if we put more air into it.

23.

divination n.

the forecast of future events or discovery of what is lost or hidden

Queen Elizabeth was impressed with Dee's powers of divination, so she appointed her spiritual consultant.

24.

doff v.

to remove or take off something, such as clothing

The gentleman doffed his hat when greeting the sophisticated woman.

25.

dogma

n.

a system of principles or tenets, as of a church

The priest declared that the church's dogma should be followed without question.

26.

doldrums

n.

a state of inactivity or stagnation, as in business or art

The government tried to do something to jump start the economy and bring it out of the doldrums.

27.

domicile

n.

the place where one lives

Stephanie required only a humble domicile and simple meals to keep herself content.

28.

don

v.

to put on or dress in

On graduation day, we all donned long, black robes for the ceremony.

29.

dour

adj.

sullen; gloomy

My aunt's terminally dour expression dissuaded us from seeking her company.

30.

dowry

n.

the property which a wife brings to her husband in marriage

The wealthy bride's family paid a huge dowry to her husband's family, following the customs of the time.

31.

droll

adj.

amusing in an odd way; whimsically humorous

The droll old man was constantly saying strange and ridiculous things that made us laugh.

32.

dross

n.

waste matter; refuse

After smelting the iron ore, the blacksmiths skimmed off the dross that had formed on the layer of molten metal.

WEEK 1
WEEK 2
WEEK 3
WEEK 4
WEEK 5
WEEK 6
WEEK 7
WEEK 8
WEEK 9
WEEK 10

ADVANCED

33.

duress n.

compulsion by threat or force; coercion; constraint

The heiress was held under duress by the kidnappers who wanted her parents to pay a ransom for their daughter's life.

34.

ecclesiastical adj.

of or pertaining to the church or the clergy; not secular

The minister wrote four volumes of ecclesiastical history focusing on our small, religious town.

35.

educe v.

to bring out a response; to deduce

From what I have been able to educe from my tight-lipped friend, we can expect a difficult test next week.

36.

effete adj.

depleted of vitality; indulgent and decadent

Americans have grown so effete that they no longer riot when the government wastes their tax dollars.

37.

efficacious adj.

effective

While efficacious for curing mild coughs, this medication won't work for serious throat infections.

38.

effigy n.

a representation or image, esp. sculptured, as on a monument

The mayor was hanged in effigy in the town square.

39.

effrontery n.

shameless or impudent boldness; barefaced audacity

How dare you have the effrontery to call me by my first name in front of my students?!

40.

egregious adj.

extraordinary in some bad way; glaring; flagrant

Though your laziness may seem innocuous now, you will feel its egregious effects later in life.

41.

egress n.

any place of exit

The back door served as our only point of egress since every other door seemed to be locked from the outside.

42.

embargo n.

authoritative stoppage of foreign commerce or of any special trade

The U.S. imposed an embargo on scrap metal exports to Japan in an effort to cut off the supply of raw materials to that country.

43.

emblazon v.

to set forth publicly or in glowing terms

The gleaming shield was emblazoned with a colorful family crest and coat of arms.

44.

emporium n.

a bazaar or shop.

Giorgio Armani has built quite an emporium, complete with his entire designer collections.

45.

encomium n.

a formal expression of high praise; eulogy

The encomium written about the President praised his commitment towards changing America for the better.

46.

endue v.

to endow with some quality, gift, or grace, usually spiritual

The religious leader endued his followers with special wisdom because of their faith in him.

47.

ennui n.

a feeling of utter weariness and discontent resulting from satiety or lack of interest; boredom

We could not shake the incredible sense of ennui while doing the menial task of separating the white beans from the red ones.

48.

epicurean adj.

devoted to sensual pleasure, esp. the enjoyment of good food and drink

The wealthy men, used to epicurean feasts, scoffed at the peanut butter and jelly sandwiches that were served.

WEEK 1
WEEK 2
WEEK 3
WEEK 4
WEEK 5
WEEK 6
WEEK 7
WEEK 8
WEEK 9
WEEK 10

ADVANCED

49.

epigram n.

any witty, ingenious, or pointed
saying tersely expressed

Grandma locked herself in a room to
compose an epigram for her
headstone.

50.

escapade n.

a reckless adventure or wild prank

Janine's father punished her severely
for her reckless escapade with his
brand new Porsche.

A. Fill in the appropriate words using the clues below.

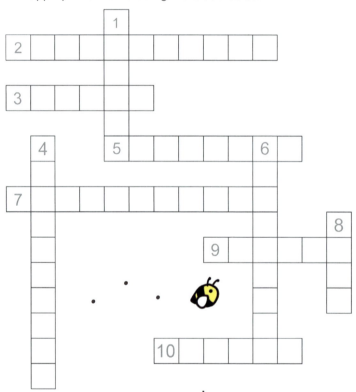

across:

2) adj. disagreeing with the majority opinion;
causing divisiveness
3) n. an authoritative and formal pronouncement
5) n. a reckless adventure or wild prank
7) adj. effective
9) adj. depleted of vitality; indulgent and
decadent
10) v. to be a mark or sign of; indicate

down:

1) v. to strip of covering, esp. foliage
4) n. shameless or impudent boldness;
barefaced audacity
6) v. to cause to lose affection, sympathy or
support
8) v. to hold as an opinion; think

B. Match the words on the left with their appropriate definitions on the right.

A. deign _____ 1. v. to deem worthy of notice or account; to condescend

B. demur _____ 2. n. a division into two opposing parts

C. deprecate _____ 3. n. the place where one lives

D. diatribe _____ 4. n. authoritative stoppage of foreign commerce or of any special trade

E. dichotomy _____ 5. adj. tending to cause delay

F. dilatory _____ 6. n. an amateur who engages in an activity without serious intentions

G. dilettante _____ 7. n. a feeling of utter weariness and discontent resulting from satiety or lack of interest; boredom

H. disingenuous _____ 8. n. a bitter, sharply abusive denunciation, attack, or criticism

I. disparity _____ 9. n. a representation or image, esp. sculptured, as on a monument

J. distend _____ 10. v. to stretch out or expand in every direction

K. dogma _____ 11. n. lack of similarity or equality; inequality; difference

L. domicile _____ 12. adj. devoted to sensual pleasure, esp. the enjoyment of good food and drink

M. duress _____ 13. adj. lacking in frankness, candor, or sincerity; falsely or hypocritically ingenuous; insincere

N. ecclesiastical _____ 14. n. compulsion by threat or force; coercion; constraint

O. efficacious _____ 15. n. a system of principles or tenets, as of a church

P. effigy _____ 16. adj. of or pertaining to the church or the clergy; not secular

Q. egregious _____ 17. adj. extraordinary in some bad way; glaring; flagrant

R. embargo _____ 18. v. to express disapproval of; to show contempt for, belittle

S. ennui _____ 19. v. to object to, often in a coy or flirtatious way

T. epicurean _____ 20. adj. effective

WEEK 1
WEEK 2
WEEK 3
WEEK 4
WEEK 5
WEEK 6
WEEK 7
WEEK 8
WEEK 9
WEEK 10

ADVANCED

300pts

100pts

Week 4

fiat

herald

**"Don't be afraid to be amazing."
- Andy Offutt Irwin**

noun

verb

1.
eschew
v.

to avoid

Our government will eschew force for as long as possible and use the military only as a last resort.

2.
ethereal
adj.

light, airy; heavenly

We thought the ethereal music was truly coming from heaven, until we saw the harpist sitting in the living room.

3.
eugenic
adj.

relating to the development of racial purity and desirable offspring

Much eugenic research conducted in the nineteenth century erroneously concluded that some races were more intelligent than others.

4.
evanescent
adj.

fleeting; likely to vanish

Unfortunately, snowflakes are only evanescent beauties because they disintegrate the moment you touch them.

5.
excise
v.

to remove by cutting out

The doctor decided she should excise the tumor since it was malignant.

6.
excommunicate
v.

to cut off or exclude from the benefits of a church, as punishment

The British king was excommunicated from the church for getting a divorce and so decided to start his own church.

7.
excoriate
v.

to denounce or berate severely; flay verbally

She excoriated her young child for running into the middle of the street and almost being hit by a semi-truck.

8.
execrable
adj.

deserving hate; of extremely inferior quality

No one should tolerate the execrable housing conditions of the inner city slums.

WEEK 1
WEEK 2
WEEK 3
WEEK 4
WEEK 5
WEEK 6
WEEK 7
WEEK 8
WEEK 9
WEEK 10

ADVANCED

9.

exhume
v.

to dig out of the earth (what has been buried)

The medical examiner wanted to exhume the victim's body because of new evidence in the murder case.

10.

exorcise
v.

to cast out (demons, for example) by religious or magical means

The brothers, undecided about how to exorcise the demons in the house, hired a Catholic priest and a voodoo expert.

11.

expiate
v.

to make amends or repayment for

The churchgoer tried to expiate her sins by saying one thousand Hail Marys.

12.

expostulate
v.

to discuss with someone in a reasoned manner, hoping to dissuade

The scientific community expostulated with the government about global warming but could not convince it of the severity of the problem.

13.

extant
adj.

still existing and known

There are only two species of the original thirty still extant; the rest have presumably died off.

14.

extensible
adj.

capable of being thrust out or extended

The telescope looks compact but is extensible to three times its current length.

15.

extenuate
v.

to represent (a fault, offense, etc.) as less serious

The defendant tried to explain that the circumstances extenuated the crime; she had no choice but to commit murder.

16.

extirpate
v.

to remove or destroy totally; do away with; exterminate

The entire ecosystem was extirpated when the fire killed half the animals and destroyed most of the trees in the forest.

17.
extrude
v.

to push or thrust out, especially through a small opening

The volcanic action extruded molten rock.

18.
factious
adj.

causing disagreement, usually between members of a group

Our relationship as colleagues was factious; we argued whenever we saw each other and could not agree on a single point.

19.
fallow
adj.

characterized by inactivity, especially referring to land left unplanted for a season

The farmers left the field fallow for the next three crop cycles and began to cultivate it only after they thought it was ready.

20.
fatalism
n.

the belief in fate

Those who believe in fatalism essentially believe that every single event is predetermined.

21.
feint
n.

any sham, pretense, or deceptive movement

The agile soccer player did a quick feint to the left and then passed the ball to a teammate to his right.

22.
felicitous
adj.

admirably appropriate for the occasion; full of happiness

Christmas in my household is a felicitous time, full of joy, presents, and good food.

23.
fetish
n.

an object that receives reverence

We collected many fetishes from our trip to Africa, items highly valued by the elders of the tribes we encountered.

24.
fiat
n.

a decree or authorization

In Rome, every first born was required by fiat to fight in the Roman army; no price could be paid to excuse the young man from his duty.

WEEK 1
WEEK 2
WEEK 3
WEEK 4
WEEK 5
WEEK 6
WEEK 7
WEEK 8
WEEK 9
WEEK 10

ADVANCED

25.
fiduciary n.
a person who is entrusted with property or assets

My sister, a corporate lawyer, was named the fiduciary of the estate since we all knew she had the best legal sense.

26.
filch v.
to steal (esp. something of small value); pilfer

She filched the fifty cents lying on her brother's dresser drawer.

27.
filibuster n.
a delaying tactic used in attempt to obstruct legislation

Senator Johnson's filibuster took the better part of the day and delayed the vote until the following week.

28.
foible n.
a personal weakness or failing

One of my personal foibles is my tendency to obsess over getting everything perfect at the cost of wasting too much time.

29.
foist v.
to pass off as genuine or worthy; to impose something unwanted or inappropriate

She tried to foist her annoying dinner date on me, but I wasn't interested in him either.

30.
fop n.
a man who is obsessed with and vain about his clothing

The Prince was such a fop that he had a new suit tailor-made for himself every day.

31.
foray n.
a venture outside of one's usual field; a sudden military attack

The author swore that this novel was to be her last foray into the mystery romance genre and that she would return to her specialty of suspense thrillers.

32.
forensic n.
pertaining to laws of public debate

Forensic examination of the bullets and blood splatters indicated murder and not suicide.

33.

forlorn
adj.

lonely, sad, desolate

The forlorn man had lost his home and all his possessions in a fire that had swept through his neighborhood.

34.

forswear
v.

to renounce upon oath

Shockingly, the priest forswore his beliefs in front of hundreds of journalists.

35.

forte
n.

a strong point

Since writing was not my forte, I asked my teacher to edit my college application essays before I sent them.

36.

fulcrum
n.

the support on or against which a lever rests, or the point about which it turns

We used a book as a fulcrum for the lever when we could find nothing else to prop it up.

37.

fulminate
v.

to erupt explosively

His mother fulminated at the idea of his dropping out of medical school to pursue acting.

38.

fulsome
adj.

offensive from excess of praise or commendation

We became suspicious when the used car salesman began giving us insincere, fulsome praise.

39.

furlough
n.

a temporary absence of a soldier or sailor by permission of the commanding officer

The major granted the private a furlough so that the private could return home to attend his grandmother's funeral.

40.

galvanize
v.

to arouse to awareness or action

With a stirring speech, the leader was able to galvanize even those people who had been apathetic about the issue.

WEEK 1
WEEK 2
WEEK 3
WEEK 4
WEEK 5
WEEK 6
WEEK 7
WEEK 8
WEEK 9
WEEK 10

ADVANCED

41.

gamut

n.

the whole range or sequence

Upon hearing that I had won the race, I experienced a whole gamut of emotions, from prideful happiness to selfless sympathy for the opposition.

42.

garner

v.

to collect or gather

The famous actress once again garnered awards and praise for her convincing screen portrayal.

43.

genteel

adj.

well-bred or refined

The genteel Southern gentleman was well educated, wealthy and chivalrous: all in all, the perfect man.

44.

gentile

n.

any group of people not Jewish

Throughout history, there has been considerable tension between Jews and gentiles.

45.

germane

adj.

relevant

This premise is germane to my argument; in fact, if you don't grasp it, there is no way you will understand the conclusion.

46.

gesticulate

v.

to make gestures or motions when speaking or in place of speech

As the student gesticulated widely in class, she nearly poked another student in the eye and knocked over her own glass of water.

47.

gibe

n.

taunt, or derisive mark; (v.) to utter taunts or reproaches

My brother always adds a little gibe at the end of an argument just to get in the last word.

48.

glib

adj.

showing little thought or concern; offhanded and casual in speech, sometimes reflecting insincerity or superficiality

Carrie makes glib generalizations about relationships and love that sound good but really don't mean much at all.

49.
gourmand   n.
a connoisseur of good food; a glutton

The gourmand, well-educated in all things food-related, proved his appreciation by eating platefuls of everything in sight.

50.
herald   v.
to proclaim; announce; (n.) a person who carries or proclaims important news; a messenger

The faraway sound of the bugle heralded great things to come, including the army's victory over the enemy.

A. Fill in the appropriate words using the clues below.

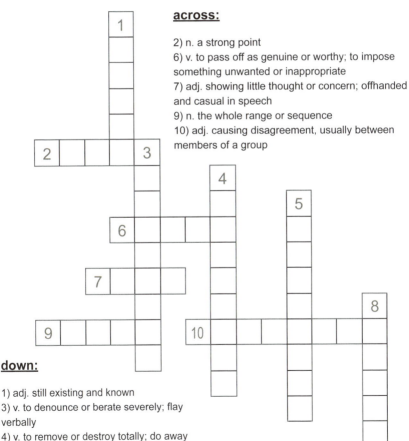

across:

2) n. a strong point
6) v. to pass off as genuine or worthy; to impose something unwanted or inappropriate
7) adj. showing little thought or concern; offhanded and casual in speech
9) n. the whole range or sequence
10) adj. causing disagreement, usually between members of a group

down:

1) adj. still existing and known
3) v. to denounce or berate severely; flay verbally
4) v. to remove or destroy totally; do away with; exterminate
5) n. a person who is entrusted with property or assets
8) v. to avoid

WEEK 1
WEEK 2
WEEK 3
WEEK 4
WEEK 5
WEEK 6
WEEK 7
WEEK 8
WEEK 9
WEEK 10

ADVANCED

B. Match the words on the left with their appropriate definitions on the right.

A. ethereal _____ 1. v. to renounce upon oath

B. evanescent _____ 2. v. to collect or gather

C. execrable _____ 3. adj. lonely, sad, desolate

D. exhume _____ 4. v. to represent (a fault, offense, etc.) as less serious

E. expiate _____ 5. v. to make amends or repayment for

F. expostulate _____ 6. v. to make gestures or motions when speaking or in place of speech

G. extenuate _____ 7. v. to discuss with someone in a reasoned manner, hoping to dissuade

H. extrude _____ 8. n. a venture outside of one's usual field; a sudden military attack

I. fallow _____ 9. v. to dig out of the earth (what has been buried)

J. felicitous _____ 10. adj. deserving hate; of extremely inferior quality

K. fiat _____ 11. adj. fleeting; likely to vanish

L. foible _____ 12. v. to push or thrust out, especially through a small opening

M. foray _____ 13. n. a decree or authorization

N. forlorn _____ 14. n. a personal weakness or failing

O. forswear _____ 15. adj. characterized by inactivity, especially referring to land left unplanted for a season

P. fulsome _____ 16. adj. admirably appropriate for the occasion; full of happiness

Q. galvanize _____ 17. adj. offensive from excess of praise or commendation

R. garner _____ 18. v. to arouse to awareness or action

S. germane _____ 19. adj. relevant

T. gesticulate _____ 20. adj. light, airy; heavenly

300pts

100pts

Week 5

iota

imbibe

 "There are no speed limits on the road to excellence."
- David W. Johnson

noun

verb

Start   Restart

 A

 B

1.
hirsute
adj.

having a hairy covering

The hirsute creature came into plain view and disappeared again so quickly that the only evidence we had of him was several strands of long, brown hair.

2.
histrionic
adj.

overly dramatic; hysterical

The woman's histrionic display outside the restaurant drew a large, amused crowd full of people wondering why she was crying.

3.
hoary
adj.

ancient; gray or white with age

Santa Claus is well known for his hoary beard, portly body, and friendly disposition.

4.
iconoclast
n.

one who rebels against and attacks the institutions of society, especially religious symbols

The rock singer, ever the iconoclast, reinvented herself once again in ways that shocked the general public.

5.
ignoble
adj.

low in character or purpose

The businessman stole money from the poor for his own ignoble purposes, so he definitely deserves to go to jail.

6.
imbibe
v.

to drink or take in

During dinner, we imbibed what seemed to be gallons of apple cider.

7.
impalpable
adj.

imperceptible to the touch

The differences in the two fabrics were impalpable, so we were shocked to find that one cost four times as much as the other.

8.
impeachable
adj.

capable of being criticized

We debated whether President Bush's actions were, in fact, impeachable according to the standard set in the Constitution.

9.

impecunious   adj.

having no money

The college student returned home impecunious and had to beg his wealthy father for an advance of money.

10.

impend   v.

to be imminent

The villagers were warned that the attack of the British army was impending.

11.

implacable   adj.

unable to be soothed

The two families were implacable foes until their daughter ran away with the other family's son.

12.

importune   v.

to harass with persistent demands or entreaties

By repeatedly sending letters to his office, the student lobbyist importuned the Dean of the School to make certain curriculum changes.

13.

impropriety   n.

the state or quality of being unfit, unseemly, or inappropriate

The impropriety of drunken behavior always dissuaded Gloria from drinking alcohol.

14.

impugn   v.

to attack one's character with arguments, insinuations, or accusations

As the campaign got uglier and more brutal, each side began to viciously impugn the other candidate.

15.

impunity   n.

exemption from punishment, penalty or harm; the perception of such exemption

Because of the police strike going on, the usually law-abiding citizens broke the law with impunity.

16.

impute   v.

to attribute

People impute great cleverness to foxes, but that reputation may only be because cartoons portray them in such a way.

WEEK 1
WEEK 2
WEEK 3
WEEK 4
WEEK 5
WEEK 6
WEEK 7
WEEK 8
WEEK 9
WEEK 10

ADVANCED

17.
incarnation   n.

a physical manifestation of one's personality or of an abstract idea or spiritual being

Dr. Jones was the incarnation of all that the small community had dreamed of in a physician, available at all times of the day and night.

18.
incendiary   adj.

tending to arouse angry emotions

Most countries would put you in jail and throw away the key if you made such incendiary comments!

19.
inculcate   v.

to instill ideas or values

Boarding schools spend a great deal of time trying to inculcate values such as loyalty and honesty in their students.

20.
incumbent   adj.

imposed as an obligation or duty; currently holding a political office

The incumbent senator had the benefit of already having a record in the Senate, and was easily reelected.

21.
indict   v.

to declare chargeable with crime

The defendant was accused and indicted of grand theft auto.

22.
indigent   adj.

lacking food, clothing, and other necessities of life because of poverty; needy; poor; impoverished; (n.) a person who is indigent

Sadly, many people became indigent when the plant closed its doors and fired all its workers.

23.
inebriate   v.

to make drunk; to intoxicate; to exhilarate or stupefy

The man was inebriated by his incredible success.

24.
ineffable   adj.

unutterable; cannot be put into words

When they were pronounced man and wife at the altar, she looked upon her new husband with ineffable tenderness.

25.

inane

adj.

silly; foolish

The silly boy often made inane suggestions during class, angering the teacher.

26.

inestimable

adj.

of immeasurable value or worth

This resource was of inestimable importance to me, for it alone helped me achieve a perfect score.

27.

inexorable

adj.

unrelenting; not capable of being persuaded

My teenaged daughter was inexorable in her quest to borrow the car tonight, so finally my wife relented.

28.

infernal

adj.

akin to or befitting hell or its occupants

The furnace seemed an infernal place to the new boiler room employees-- incredibly hot and filled with thick clouds of soot.

29.

infringe

v.

to trespass upon, especially upon one's rights

The Constitution does not allow the government to infringe on citizens' rights unfairly.

30.

infuse

v.

to instill idea, introduce fluids, or inculcate principles

Ever since I was a little girl, my mother has infused in me principles by which she hopes I will live for the rest of my life.

31.

ingrate

n.

someone who is ungrateful

The young ingrate never once said "Thank you" to her grandmother, who had raised her from infancy.

32.

inimical

adj.

harmful; hostile (like an enemy)

She had a reputation as an inimical book critic who was ten times more willing to criticize than to praise.

WEEK 1
WEEK 2
WEEK 3
WEEK 4
WEEK 5
WEEK 6
WEEK 7
WEEK 8
WEEK 9
WEEK 10

ADVANCED

33.

inimitable   adj.

so good that it cannot be copied

The actress had an inimitable screen quality that many generations of younger actresses have tried to copy but failed.

34.

inopportune   adj.

unsuitable or inconvenient, especially as to time

Her inopportune appearance at a party to which she had not been invited made the others feel awkward.

35.

insolvent   adj.

bankrupt, unable to pay one's debts

Jed was once a millionaire, but now he is insolvent and cannot even afford his rent.

36.

insouciant   adj.

unconcerned in a carefree way; nonchalant

The young man had such an insouciant attitude that none of the girls thought he was interested.

37.

insular   adj.

isolated or narrow-minded; detached from the rest of the world

The insular community had no contact with the outside world and developed its own bizarre society.

38.

inter   v.

to bury

The woman could not stand to see her deceased husband buried and became hysterical, begging the grounds keeper not to inter him.

39.

interdict   v.

to use legal or religious authority to prohibit a person's activities, especially entry into a country

The FBI had a role in interdicting spies trying to pass U.S. secrets to the Soviet Union.

40.

interlocutor   n.

one who takes part as a mediator in a conversation or oral discussion

The interlocutor at the conference explained to us his own views and presented the issue at hand.

41.

interloper
n.

one who interferes or intrudes

While we were chatting at the restaurant, an interloper sitting nearby kept adding his own comments to our discussion.

42.

interpolation
n.

an insertion into a text or conversation; to change (or falsify) a text by adding material

With the help of her brother's frequent interpolations, her story was eventually told.

43.

innuendo
n.

an indirect suggestion of something, usually negative

American television thrives on sexual innuendo and wordplay that would have been scandalous forty years ago.

44.

inure
v.

to harden or toughen by use or exposure; to become accustomed to something negative

Having lived in Alaska for twenty years, I must admit I am inured to the cold.

45.

invective
n.

an utterance intended to criticize or denounce in an abusive way

The angered baseball manager screamed invectives at his players after they had lost nine straight games.

46.

inveigh
v.

to protest strongly or attack vehemently with words; rail (usually fol. by against)

The students inveighed against the amount of homework that the teacher gave them to do over the break.

47.

inveterate
adj.

habitual

Stacey was an inveterate liar and could tell a string of untruths without a moment's hesitation.

48.

invidious
adj.

causing animosity; showing or feeling envy

Her invidious comments inevitably gave rise to feelings of jealousy and discrimination between the two sisters.

WEEK 1
WEEK 2
WEEK 3
WEEK 4
WEEK 5
WEEK 6
WEEK 7
WEEK 8
WEEK 9
WEEK 10

ADVANCED

49.

iota

n.

a small or insignificant mark or part

Every iota of information can be valuable when playing Trivial Pursuit or Scrabble.

50.

iridescent

adj.

exhibiting a display of lustrous or rainbowlike colors

If you look carefully, you will see soap bubbles are actually iridescent rather than clear in color.

A. Fill in the appropriate words using the clues below.

across:

1) v. to intoxicate
4) v. to bury
7) adj. causing animosity; showing or feeling envy
8) adj. needy; poor; impoverished
9) n. one who rebels against and attacks the institutions of society, especially religious symbols

down:

2) v. to harass with persistent demands or entreaties
3) adj. overly dramatic; hysterical
4) adj. unconcerned in a carefree way; nonchalant
5) adj. having no money
6) v. to protest strongly or attack vehemently with words (usually fol. by against)

B. Match the words on the left with their appropriate definitions on the right.

A. hirsute _____ 1. adj. tending to arouse angry emotions

B. imbibe _____ 2. n. one who takes part as a mediator in a conversation or oral discussion

C. impalpable _____ 3. adj. habitual

D. impend _____ 4. v. to drink or take in

E. impugn _____ 5. adj. harmful; hostile (like an enemy)

F. impunity _____ 6. n. an utterance intended to criticize or denounce in an abusive way

G. incendiary _____ 7. adj. bankrupt, unable to pay one's debts

H. incumbent _____ 8. adj. unrelenting; not capable of being persuaded

I. indict _____ 9. n. exemption from punishment, penalty or harm; the perception of such exemption

J. ineffable _____ 10. v. to be imminent

K. inexorable _____ 11. v. to trespass upon, especially upon one's rights

L. infringe _____ 12. adj. imperceptible to the touch

M. inimical _____ 13. v. to attack one's character with arguments, insinuations, or accusations

N. insolvent _____ 14. adj. unutterable; cannot be put into words

O. insular _____ 15. v. to declare chargeable with crime

P. interlocutor _____ 16. n. a small or insignificant mark or part

Q. inure _____ 17. adj. imposed as an obligation or duty; currently holding a political office

R. invective _____ 18. adj. isolated or narrow-minded; detached from the rest of the world

S. inveterate _____ 19. adj. having a hairy covering

T. iota _____ 20. v. to harden or toughen by use or exposure; to become accustomed to something negative

WEEK 1
WEEK 2
WEEK 3
WEEK 4
WEEK 5
WEEK 6
WEEK 7
WEEK 8
WEEK 9
WEEK 10

ADVANCED

300pts

100pts

Week 6

mete

liturgy

"Success is the sum of small efforts, repeated day in and day out."
- Robert Collier

verb

noun

Start   Restart

 A

 B

1.

jibe   v.

to be in agreement or conformity

Answering questions about her personal history did not jibe with her mom's view of parenting children.

2.

jingoism   n.

zealous patriotism; the belief that one's country is far superior to all others

During World War II, a paranoia partially based in jingoism resulted in the internment of thousands of Japanese-Americans.

3.

jocund   adj.

cheerful; merry; blithe; glad

A jocund person would be welcomed in any gathering, whether lively or moody.

4.

juggernaut   n.

overwhelming force that seems to crush everything in its path

When it came to wrestling, he was a juggernaut, winning every match easily.

5.

junta   n.

a council or assembly that deliberates in secret upon the affairs of government

The military junta formed to overthrow the current regime but were found out before any serious damage was done.

6.

juxtapose   v.

to place close together, especially to show contrast or highlight similarities

Literary writers often juxtapose two opposite feelings to give readers a sense of the emotional struggle of the characters.

7.

jurisprudence   n.

the philosophy of law, as taught in law schools

Lawyers have "JD" degrees, and are known as Doctors of Jurisprudence.

8.

kaleidoscopic   adj.

characterized by a constantly changing set of colors (or events)

The room was painted a kaleidoscopic array of colors and gave me a headache every time I walked in.

WEEK 1
WEEK 2
WEEK 3
WEEK 4
WEEK 5
WEEK 6
WEEK 7
WEEK 8
WEEK 9
WEEK 10

ADVANCED

9.
knavery n.
dishonest or crafty dealing; trickery or mischief

Any attempts at knavery in school will be swiftly punished with expulsion.

10.
labyrinth n.
a maze

Bill found the county Department of Building and Safety to be a labyrinth of rules and regulations.

11.
lachrymose adj.
suggestive of or tending to cause tears; mournful

The movie was so sad that it made everyone become as weepy as a lachrymose teenage girl.

12.
lackadaisical adj.
lacking vitality or interest; lazy in a dreamy way

A lackadaisical disposition will prevent one from achieving his goals.

13.
laggard adj.
falling behind; (n.) one who lags, falls behind

The laggard eventually got lost from the pack, so we had to backtrack to search for him.

14.
latitude n.
freedom from narrow restrictions; freedom of action, opinion, etc.

The teacher gave lots of latitude when grading the essays.

15.
lassitude n.
a feeling of weariness or diminished energy

It was tough to overcome the students' lassitude in trying to teach them yet again the principles of grammar.

16.
legerdemain n.
trickery; deception

The magician amazed the children with his feats of legerdemain.

17.

leviathan n.

any large animal, as a whale; anything unusually large, especially a ship

The giant squid in the museum is a true leviathan; one of its tentacles is as tall as a house.

18.

levy v.

to impose and collect (especially taxes) by force or threat of force

The British levied taxes on the American colonists without giving them representation in Parliament.

19.

liaison n.

one that maintains communication; a close relationship, connection, or link; an adulterous relationship; an affair

The French liaison acted as a go-between for the English and Italian governments.

20.

licentious adj.

lacking moral discipline or ignoring legal restraint, especially in sexual conduct

The licentious young man finally got his due when he was arrested by police for lewd and unlawful activity.

21.

linguist n.

one who is acquainted with several languages

The linguist in the Language Department was fluent in six different languages!

22.

litany n.

a prayer involving repetition of verses; any repetitive list

The lawyer read a litany of complaints made by the patient that appeared to go on for twenty pages.

23.

liturgy n.

a ritual

The church attendees were not used to the new forms of liturgy decided upon by the cardinals in Rome.

24.

loquacious adj.

talking or tending to talk much or freely; talkative; chattering; babbling; garrulous

The little five year old was so loquacious that the baby-sitter could not wait until the child's naptime so there would be some peace and quiet.

WEEK 1
WEEK 2
WEEK 3
WEEK 4
WEEK 5
WEEK 6
WEEK 7
WEEK 8
WEEK 9
WEEK 10

ADVANCED

25.
lugubrious adj.

mournful, dismal, or gloomy, esp. in an affected, exaggerated, or unrelieved manner

Some clowns paint their faces with joyful smiles while others choose to wear a lugubrious frown.

26.
maladroit adj.

lacking in adroitness; unskillful; awkward; bungling; tactless

The large maladroit man often walked into shelves knocking over small, fragile knickknacks.

27.
mawkish adj.

excessively sentimental; sickening or insipid

The woman spoke in a mawkish manner about the young, attractive actor who had won her heart with his sweet yet manly demeanor.

28.
melée n.

a confused, rowdy mingling

The melée of Christmas shoppers always makes we want to hide in my house during the holidays.

29.
meliorate v.

to make better or improve, as in quality or social or physical condition

The Simpson family meliorated their infuriated neighbors by inviting them over for their Sunday barbecue.

30.
mendacious adj.

dishonest; untrue

The teenager was an immoral and mendacious person who lied to everyone about her whereabouts.

31.
mendicant n.

a beggar living on alms

Many people living on the street quickly turn into mendicants, pleading and hoping to survive on the kindness of strangers.

32.
menial adj.

related to the type of work that would be done by a servant, especially that requiring physical labor

The factory worker found his task of sewing buttons all day to be menial work.

33.

metaphysical adj.

philosophical; based on abstract reasoning; supernatural

The metaphysical poetry of John Donne is characterized by the union of argument, wit, and pathos.

34.

mete v.

to distribute as if by measuring

The teacher meted out the punishment to all those who broke class rules.

35.

meticulous adj.

marked by extreme or excessive care in the consideration or treatment of detail

The wedding planner was extremely meticulous, a trait that helped her succeed at her job.

36.

mettle n.

courage and fortitude

Oliver was renowned for his mettle, facing the enemy fearlessly in the open field.

37.

mien n.

the external appearance or manner of a person

He is a man of noble mien, who truly believes in his principles.

38.

minatory adj.

menacing

The Minotaur, with the head of a bull and body of a man, was a minatory creature, killing all who wandered into its lair.

39.

minion n.

a servile follower

Many minions followed the pop singer as she toured the country.

40.

ministration n.

the act or process of aiding someone

Pastor Frank gave spiritual ministrations to the farmers who had suffered during the flood.

WEEK 1
WEEK 2
WEEK 3
WEEK 4
WEEK 5
WEEK 6
WEEK 7
WEEK 8
WEEK 9
WEEK 10

ADVANCED

41.
miscreant
n.

a villain

Every movie has a hero who must deal not only with villains but also with assorted miscreants.

42.
misogyny
n.

hatred of women

A true misogynist will be someone who treats women as though they are worthless.

43.
modicum
n.

a moderate or small amount

It takes only a modicum of effort to become proficient in vocabulary skills.

44.
modish
adj.

fashionable

Modish models wear the latest designer fashions of Paris.

45.
moratorium
n.

a suspension, usually temporary, of some action or activity

Several countries placed a moratorium on weapons production until a new treaty could be signed that would set reasonable limits on each nation's arsenal.

46.
moribund
adj.

on the point of dying

The doctor told the moribund patient the diagnosis: the patient had only a week to live.

47.
motif
n.

a repeated theme, especially in music or architecture

The motif of the song was played several times to emphasize that the music reflected the sadness of the composer.

48.
motley
adj.

composed of heterogeneous or inharmonious elements

A motley crowd of teens, adults, and seniors all came to watch the premiere of the new movie.

49.

myriad
n.

a vast indefinite number; made up of numerous diverse elements

A myriad of stars sparkle in the clear night sky over the lonely valley.

50.

nadir
n.

the lowest point; point of greatest adversity or despair

Unfortunately, the company hit the nadir of its existence last quarter, losing millions of dollars in bad investments.

A. Fill in the appropriate words using the clues below.

down:

1) n. the philosophy of law, as taught in law schools
2) n. hatred of women
3) n. the act or process of aiding someone
4) n. trickery, deception

across:

3) adj. philosophical; based on abstract reasoning; supernatural
5) n. zealous patriotism; the belief that one's country is far superior to all others
6) n. any large animal, as a whale; anything unusually large, especially a ship
7) n. a ritual
8) adj. composed of heterogeneous or inharmonious elements

WEEK 1
WEEK 2
WEEK 3
WEEK 4
WEEK 5
WEEK 6
WEEK 7
WEEK 8
WEEK 9
WEEK 10

ADVANCED

B. Match the words on the left with their appropriate definitions on the right.

A. jocund   _____   1. adj. cheerful; merry; blithe; glad

B. labyrinth   _____   2. n. a maze

C. lachrymose   _____   3. v. to impose and collect (especially taxes) by force or threat of force

D. lackadaisical   _____   4. adj. talking or tending to talk much or freely; talkative; chattering; babbling; garrulous

E. latitude   _____   5. adj. lacking moral discipline or ignoring legal restraint, especially in sexual conduct

F. levy   _____   6. n. a vast indefinite number; made up of numerous diverse elements

G. licentious   _____   7. n. freedom from narrow restrictions; freedom of action, opinion, etc.

H. litany   _____   8. adj. excessively sentimental; sickening or insipid

I. loquacious   _____   9. n. the lowest point; point of greatest adversity or despair

J. lugubrious   _____ 10. adj. lacking vitality or interest; lazy in a dreamy way

K. maladroit   _____ 11. n. the external appearance or manner of a person

L. mawkish   _____ 12. n. a repeated theme, especially in music or architecture

M. mendicant   _____ 13. adj. suggestive of or tending to cause tears; mournful

N. mete   _____ 14. v. to distribute as if by measuring

O. mien   _____ 15. n. a villain

P. miscreant   _____ 16. n. a moderate or small amount

Q. modicum   _____ 17. adj. mournful, dismal, or gloomy, esp. in an affected, exaggerated, or unrelieved manner

R. motif   _____ 18. adj. lacking in adroitness; unskillful; awkward; bungling; tactless

S. myriad   _____ 19. n. a beggar, living on alms

T. nadir   _____ 20. n. a prayer involving repetition of verses; any repetitive list

300pts

100pts

Week 7

pall

paltry

"People often say that motivation doesn't last. Well, neither does bathing-- that's why we recommend it daily." - Zig Ziglar

noun

adj.

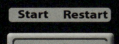

Start   Restart

A

B

1.

nascent adj.

beginning to exist or develop

We are at the nascent point in our program; we look forward to years of growth and success.

2.

neologism n.

a new word, expression, or usage

Every word in our language must have been a neologism at one time.

3.

nettle v.

to excite sensations of uneasiness or displeasure in

He was nettled constantly by his little sister whenever she wanted to play while he was doing his homework.

4.

nihilism n.

total rejection of established laws and institutions; anarchy

The revolutionaries did not want a new government so much as they wanted to express their anti-social, nihilistic ideas.

5.

nirvana n.

a place or feeling of perfect happiness

A goal for all good Eastern mystics is to reach a state of nirvana, where one is purged of all base humanity and becomes one with creation.

6.

noisome adj.

very offensive, particularly to the sense of smell

As we drove along the countryside, we quickly sensed the noisome odor of a dead skunk.

7.

non-partisan adj.

objective; not supporting or controlled by a political party, special interest group, or the like; (n.) a person who is nonpartisan

The candidate tried to be non-partisan and listen to both sides of the budget debate.

8.

nonplussed v.

to render utterly perplexed; puzzle completely

He was nonplussed by the news of the hike in taxes, so he called his congressman for an explanation.

9.

nostrum   n.

any solution which may be popular but is untested and possibly fraudulent

The little pills my grandfather purchased from the traveling salesman turned out to be a nostrum, useless for anything.

10.

nugatory   adj.

having no power or force; having little importance

His role in the theater was hardly stellar, more like a series of nugatory appearances on stage.

11.

obsequious   adj.

showing a servile readiness to fall in with the wishes or will of another

The obsequious young man bowed and said, "I am at your service, Master."

12.

obstreperous   adj.

noisy and defiant; boisterous; hard to control

Unlike the Wixburg's obstreperous children, my six children are so well behaved that hardly anyone knows they exist.

13.

obtrude   v.

to be pushed or to push oneself into undue prominence; to thrust forward

Most of my nosey neighbors stand at the fence where our yards meet, obtruding themselves into other people's lives.

14.

occlude   v.

to cause to become closed; to prevent the passage of

The muscles and nerves in his eye became so weak that his eyelid and even his pupil occluded, preventing him from seeing clearly.

15.

ocular   adj.

of or pertaining to the eye

The inventors have worked tirelessly on developing the ocular function in their robots, helping them to distinguish forms by sight.

16.

olfactory   adj.

of or pertaining to the sense of smell

The sense of smell is achieved through the use of the olfactory organ which usually, on a human, rests in the nose.

WEEK 1
WEEK 2
WEEK 3
WEEK 4
WEEK 5
WEEK 6
WEEK 7
WEEK 8
WEEK 9
WEEK 10

ADVANCED

17.

ostensibly

adv.

outwardly appearing as such; professed; pretended

The building appeared ostensibily strong, despite the fact that it had large cracks in its foundation from the last earthquake.

18.

pall

n.

a covering that darkens or obscures

A pall of despair settled over the whole crowd as the jet fighters crashed during the air show.

19.

pallor

n.

extreme or unnatural paleness

The pallor of the dead is often frightening to the living.

20.

palpitate

v.

to move with a trembling motion; to beat with rapidity

Her heart palpitated quickly when she thought she saw some real ghosts in the haunted mansion.

21.

panegyric

n.

a lofty oration or writing in praise of a person or thing; eulogy

The city councilmen published several panegyrics for the mayor on his forty years of service to the city.

22.

panoply

n.

a wide-ranging and impressive array or display

Going to the farmer's market, Greg and his wife were amazed at the panoply of fruits and vegetables available at reasonable prices.

23.

pantheon

n.

all the gods of a people considered as a group

The Greek pantheon of gods continues to be a source of inspiration to poets worldwide.

24.

paraphernalia

n.

miscellaneous articles of equipment or adornment

In the back room lay most of the sports paraphernalia that could not be used by anyone on the team.

25.

parley

v.

to have a discussion or conference, especially between enemies over terms of a truce

After they had parleyed, the student council candidates agreed not to demean each other during the election campaign.

26.

parsimonious

adj.

stingy; very ungenerous

Margaret became renowned for her parsimonious approach to spending after having argued that the prices at the 99 Cents Store were too high.

27.

paltry

adj.

very small and almost worthless; trifling

The single mother looked at her paltry paycheck and wondered how she would pay rent.

28.

patrician

adj.

of refined upbringing, manners, or taste; of senatorial or noble rank

The politicians of Ancient Rome were patricians, noble men of wealth who sought power and influence within the empire.

29.

parochial

adj.

narrowly restricted in scope or outlook

Tired of the parochial outlook of her fellow villagers, Mary dreamed of escaping to the city.

30.

peccable

adj.

capable of sinning; likely to contain error

The index for the new book on the Kennedy assassination is extensive though peccable; a tome of that size is certain to contain errors.

31.

peccadillo

n.

a minor sin or fault

His constant whistling at the most inappropriate time was a peccadillo that managed to get Theodore in trouble often with the teacher.

32.

pecuniary

adj.

of or pertaining to money

Larry could not fly out to his high school reunion for pecuniary reasons.

WEEK 1
WEEK 2
WEEK 3
WEEK 4
WEEK 5
WEEK 6
WEEK 7
WEEK 8
WEEK 9
WEEK 10

ADVANCED

33.

pedagogy n.

the science and art of teaching

Cal Tech is know for its pedagogy in the engineering fields.

34.

pellucid adj.

translucent

They were amazed at the pellucid beauty of the lake as they gazed into its depths.

35.

pendulous adj.

hanging, especially so as to swing by an attached end or part

The pendulous vines swung back and forth before us as we made our way through the thick jungle.

36.

pension n.

a periodical allowance to an individual on account of past service performed; a retirement plan

Monthly pensions received by the veterans were barely enough for them to pay their bills.

37.

penurious adj.

excessively sparing in the use of money

Mark gave up his penurious ways forever when he finally won the lottery.

38.

perambulate v.

to walk about

I perambulated around the plaza, trying to figure out what I was going to do with my free afternoon.

39.

peremptory adj.

not allowing contradiction, debate, refusal, or appeal

The general issued a peremptory command that superceded any other conflicting commands.

40.

perennial adj.

continuing though the year or through many years

The perennial repairing of the freeways was an inconvenience to commuters who drove every day.

41.

perfidy

n.

treachery

She developed a bad reputation for her perfidy because she would leak secrets of anyone around her, friend or foe.

42.

peripatetic

adj.

walking about or from place to place

The peripatetic nomad walked from city to city, trying to find a place to settle down.

43.

permutation

n.

a complete change; transformation

He created several permutations of the original painting, each one slightly different from all the others.

44.

perjure

v.

to swear falsely to; to give false testimony; to lie while under oath

He was put into jail after he perjured himself in court.

45.

petulant

adj.

unreasonably irritable and annoyed, especially when contemptuous and pouty

After Dan insulted her, Nelda left the room with a petulant toss of the head.

46.

perspicacious

adj.

having keen mental perception

Albert Einstein had a perspicacious mind and created many innovative ideas during his time.

47.

phantasm

n.

something apparently seen but having no reality, such as a ghost

The little girl's imaginary friend, "Philly," was a phantasm alleged to be a friendly, talking panda bear.

48.

philander

v.

to engage in love affairs with women

The movie star philandered with many women, breaking many hearts.

WEEK 1
WEEK 2
WEEK 3
WEEK 4
WEEK 5
WEEK 6
WEEK 7
WEEK 8
WEEK 9
WEEK 10

ADVANCED

49.

philistine   adj.

crude and unsophisticated, especially in regard to culture and the arts

Campus fraternities are noted for their philistine members who are more concerned with throwing parties than studying.

50.

picayune   adj.

of little value or importance

She couldn't believe she was being sent to jail for such a picayune infraction of the law.

A. Fill in the appropriate words using the clues below.

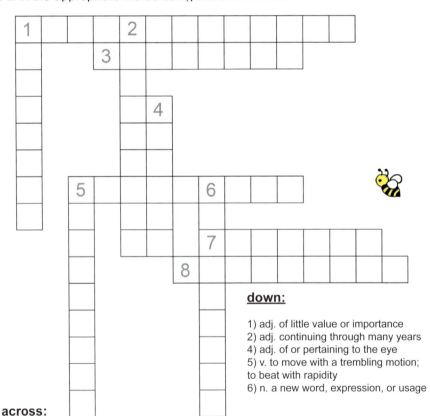

down:

1) adj. of little value or importance
2) adj. continuing through many years
4) adj. of or pertaining to the eye
5) v. to move with a trembling motion; to beat with rapidity
6) n. a new word, expression, or usage

across:

1) adj. having keen mental perception
3) adj. capable of sinning; likely to contain error
5) v. to engage in love affairs with women
7) v. to be pushed or to push oneself into undue prominence; to thrust forward
8) adj. of or pertaining to the sense of smell

B. Match the words on the left with their appropriate definitions on the right.

A. nascent   _____   1. adj. beginning to exist or develop

B. nihilism   _____   2. n. a minor sin or fault

C. noisome   _____   3. adj. crude and unsophisticated, especially in regard to culture and the arts

D. nonplussed   _____   4. n. the science and art of teaching

E. obsequious   _____   5. v. to walk about

F. obstreperous   _____   6. adj. noisy and defiant; boisterous; hard to control

G. occlude   _____   7. n. extreme or unnatural paleness

H. ostensibly   _____   8. n. treachery

I. pallor   _____   9. adj. showing a servile readiness to fall in with the wishes or will of another

J. panoply   _____ 10. v. to render utterly perplexed; puzzle completely

K. parsimonious   _____ 11. adj. very offensive, particularly to the sense of smell

L. patrician   _____ 12. adj. stingy; very ungenerous

M. peccadillo   _____ 13. adj. outwardly appearing as such; professed; pretended

N. pecuniary   _____ 14. n. a wide-ranging and impressive array or display

O. pedagogy   _____ 15. adj. of or pertaining to money

P. perambulate   _____ 16. adj. having keen mental perception

Q. peremptory   _____ 17. adj. not allowing contradiction, debate, refusal, or appeal

R. perfidy   _____ 18. adj. of refined upbringing, manners, or taste; of senatorial or noble rank

S. perspicacious   _____ 19. n. total rejection of established laws and institutions; anarchy

T. philstine   _____ 20. v. to cause to become closed; to prevent the passage of

WEEK 1
WEEK 2
WEEK 3
WEEK 4
WEEK 5
WEEK 6
WEEK 7
WEEK 8
WEEK 9
WEEK 10

ADVANCED

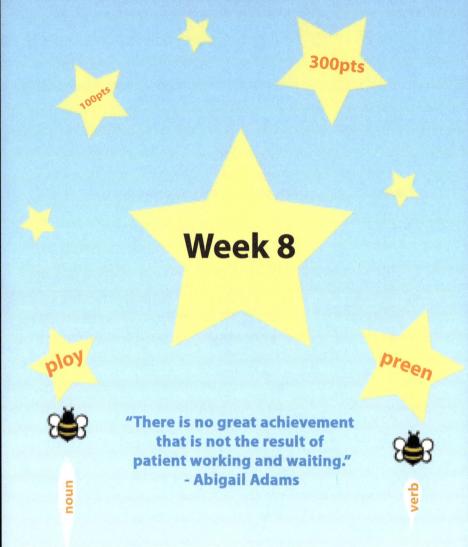

300pts

100pts

Week 8

ploy

preen

"There is no great achievement
that is not the result of
patient working and waiting."
- Abigail Adams

noun

verb

Start   Restart

A   B

1.

pilfer

v.

to steal, esp. in small quantities

Keith caught the young boy who had pilfered three bags of potato chips from the stacks.

2.

pillage

n.

open robbery, as in war

The village's inhabitants protected themselves from pillage by an elaborate system of booby traps.

3.

pittance

n.

any small portion or meager allowance

The pittance given by the stingy boss caused the workers to complain.

4.

placebo

n.

something such as medicine that has no intrinsic value, but is given to someone to appease or soothe

Even though the medicine was a placebo, the patients seemed to show miraculous improvement.

5.

platonic

adj.

beyond physical desire and tending toward the spiritual or mental

Although many suspected that Jim and Kim were dating, the pair insisted their relationship was platonic; they were "just friends."

6.

plebeian

adj.

common, unsophisticated

The plebeian citizen works ten-hour shifts and then goes home to have dinner with his wife and children and go to bed; then, he does it all again.

7.

plenary

adj.

complete in all respects, unlimited; attended by all members

The only plenary meeting of the student council was at the beginning of the year, when all the members showed up.

8.

ploy

n.

a maneuver or stratagem, as in conversation, to gain the advantage

Morris told Bryan about his ploy to beat Frank at the video game.

WEEK 1
WEEK 2
WEEK 3
WEEK 4
WEEK 5
WEEK 6
WEEK 7
WEEK 8
WEEK 9
WEEK 10

ADVANCED

9.
plumb
v.

to determine depth; to probe deeply

The marine biologist used a special sonar device to plumb the depth of the ocean.

10.
plurality
n.

a majority; a large number

The Democratic candidates in this area consistently receive the plurality of votes.

11.
pommel
v.

to beat with something thick or bulky

The desperate knight began to pommel the beast with the hilt of his sword after the blade had been broken.

12.
pontificate
v.

to speak as if one's words have ultimate authority

The teacher pontificated endlessly about binomial equations as if they were the most important concepts to mathematics.

13.
posit
v.

to present in an orderly manner

The story posited a complex moral situation for its characters.

14.
pragmatic
n.

practical; dealing with facts and actual occurrences

Joe takes a pragmatic approach to life, dealing only with necessities of living and ignoring such fuzzy notions as religion and philosophy.

15.
prate
v.

to talk at length in a foolish manner

The child prated on and on, but no one could understand what he was talking about.

16.
prattle
v.

to talk or chatter idly or meaninglessly

The annoying man always prattles with his coworkers during work time.

17.
preamble *n.*
a statement introductory to and explanatory of what follows

The Preamble to the U.S. Constitution is a brief introduction of what the Constitution is intended to do.

18.
preclude *v.*
to prevent the presence, existence, or occurrence of; make impossible

Fire drills help to preclude the panic of an actual fire.

19.
predilection *n.*
a preference for something

She has a predilection for baseball-sized jawbreakers, even though the candy is almost impossible to eat.

20.
preen *v.*
to smooth feathers; to groom or dress oneself with excessive care or pride

The mother duck preened her duckling neatly, smoothing its downy feathers to a delicate sheen.

21.
preponderence *n.*
superiority in weight, force, or importance

The preponderance of votes is against the proposal for a new landfill in the neighborhood.

22.
prescience *n.*
knowledge of events before they take place

It takes a certain degree of prescience to be a careful reader of mystery novels.

23.
presentiment *n.*
foreboding

Thornbee's presentiment that the judge would dismiss the case turned out to be accurate.

24.
prevaricate *v.*
to use ambiguous or evasive language for the purpose of deceiving or diverting attention

When asked what happened to his homework, the child prevaricated and said his dog had eaten it.

WEEK 1
WEEK 2
WEEK 3
WEEK 4
WEEK 5
WEEK 6
WEEK 7
WEEK 8
WEEK 9
WEEK 10

ADVANCED

25.

priggish   adj.

having an exaggerated and conceited sense of propriety

The priggish man looked down upon those who he thought were acting foolishly at the party.

26.

primeval   v.

belonging to the first ages

Fossils of primeval creatures unearthed by geologists reveal the forms of our most distant ancestors.

27.

privation   n.

lack of necessities, such as food or shelter

The starving children suffered great privation after the horrible drought.

28.

privy   adj.

participating with another or others in the knowledge of a secret transaction

No one was privy to the information of the homicide except the police.

29.

probity   n.

integrity and uprightness; honesty

The moral probity of the candidate made him a popular choice for president.

30.

proclivity   n.

natural or habitual inclination or tendency; predisposition

They had a proclivity toward staying up all night to do hmework instead of doing it during the day.

31.

procure   v.

to obtain, especially by special effort

The librarian insisted that the antique books be procured by a veteran administrator with experience in handling rare items.

32.

profligacy   n.

reckless and extravagant wastefulness

The profligacy of her wedding was beyond belief! Thirty thousand dollars went toward just the flower arrangements.

33.

progeny

n.

offspring

If you encounter the young progeny of a bear while you are in the woods, go in the opposite direction.

34.

proletarian

n.

a person of the lowest or poorest class; those who earn money by laboring for others

It seems that the proletarians of the world work the hardest, and earn the least money for their efforts.

35.

prolix

adj.

tediously wordy

The students skipped the prolix instructions because they wanted to begin the test as soon as possible.

36.

promenade

v.

to walk for amusement or exercise

In the olden days, couples and families would take the afternoon to promenade in the park.

37.

promontory

n.

a high point of land extending outward from the coastline into the sea

The couple wanted to have their wedding on top of a promontory so they could have the ocean as the background.

38.

propitiate

v.

to make favorably inclined; appease; conciliate

After offending the boss, Hilda tried to propitiate him by inviting him to dinner.

39.

propound

v.

to put forward ideas for consideration

The baker propounded that her pound cake was the best in the world!

40.

proscribe

v.

to reject officially something such as a teaching or a practice, with condemnation or denunciation

Cell phones are proscribed in school because they are nuisances and a source of distraction to the students during class.

WEEK 1
WEEK 2
WEEK 3
WEEK 4
WEEK 5
WEEK 6
WEEK 7
WEEK 8
WEEK 9
WEEK 10

ADVANCED

41.

proselytize   v.

to attempt to convert someone to a belief or idea, especially religious ones

Many religious groups, particularly various fundamentalist Christians, aggressively seek to proselytize others.

42.

prosy   adj.

prosaic; dull, tedious, wearisome, or commonplace

His essays were quite prosy, dull instead of inspirationally lyrical.

43.

protean   adj.

readily assuming different forms or characters; extremely variable

High school romances can be quite protean and short-lived.

44.

protégé   n.

one specially cared for and favored by another usually older person

The master's protégé is truly one of a kind, for he reached black belt at the age of 18.

45.

protocol   n.

a code of correct conduct, especially in regard to diplomacy

The protocol for dealing with an earthquake during school hours may be different from what one would do at home.

46.

proxy   n.

a person who is empowered by another to represent him or her in a given matter

When Paula was pregnant, the company hired a proxy to do her job while she nursed the baby.

47.

prude   n.

one who is excessively moral

She was teased for being a prude because she insisted on wearing long skirts and high-collared shirts.

48.

puerile   adj.

childish

The puerile man's attitude was inappropriate for the seriousness of the corporate meeting.

49.

pugnacious

adj.

combative in nature; belligerent

We thought our pug would grow up to be pugnacious, but, as it turns out, he is quite docile.

50.

puissant

adj.

possessing power

The core of the movie was a battle between three gallant knights and a puissant dragon.

WEEK 1
WEEK 2
WEEK 3
WEEK 4
WEEK 5
WEEK 6
WEEK 7
WEEK 8
WEEK 9
WEEK 10

A. Fill in the appropriate words using the clues below.

down:

1) n. open robbery, as in war
3) v. to make favorably inclined; appease
4) v. to speak as if one's words have ultimate authority

across:

2) v. to put forward ideas for consideration
5) adj. readily assuming different forms or characters; extremely variable
6) adj. beyond physical desire and tending toward the spiritual or mental
7) v. to present in an orderly manner
8) n. superiority in weight, force or importance
9) adj. belonging to the first ages
10) n. something such as medicine that has no intrinsic value, but is given to someone to appease or soothe

B. Match the words on the left with their appropriate definitions on the right.

A. pilfer _____ 1. n. any small portion or meager allowance

B. pittance _____ 2. n. a person of the lowest or poorest class; those who earn money by laboring for others

C. plebeian _____ 3. adj. common, unsophisticated

D. ploy _____ 4. n. lack of necessities, such as food or shelter

E. pontificate _____ 5. adj. combative in nature; belligerent

F. preclude _____ 6. adj. readily assuming different forms or characters; extremely variable

G. predilection _____ 7. adj. childish

H. prescience _____ 8. n. natural or habitual inclination or tendency; predisposition

I. prevaricate _____ 9. v. to steal, esp. in small quantities

J. privation _____ 10. v. to reject officially something such as a teaching or a practice, with condemnation or denunciation

K. probity _____ 11. v. to use ambiguous or evasive language for the purpose of deceiving or diverting attention

L. proclivity _____ 12. n. a maneuver or stratagem, as in conversation, to gain the advantage

M. procure _____ 13. n. integrity and uprightness; honesty

N. proletarian _____ 14. v. to speak as if one's words have ultimate authority

O. proscribe _____ 15. v. to prevent the presence, existence, or occurrence of; make impossible

P. proselytize _____ 16. v. to obtain, especially by special effort

Q. protean _____ 17. n. knowledge of events before they take place

R. proxy _____ 18. n. a person who is empowered by another to represent him or her in a given matter

S. puerile _____ 19. v. to attempt to convert someone to a belief or idea, especially religious ones

T. pugnacious _____ 20. n. a preference for something

300pts

100pts

Week 9

pyre

staid

"'I can't do it' never yet
accomplished anything;
'I will try' has performed wonders."
- George P. Burnham

noun

adj.

Start   Restart

A

B

1.
punctilious adj.

extremely attentive to details, esp. those related to formalities or proper conduct

Paul was punctilious in the way he analyzed the balance sheet for the past three years.

2.
purloin v.

to steal, often in violation of trust

The man reached over and purloined a five dollar bill from the donation jar.

3.
purported adj.

reputed or claimed; alleged

It was purported that the Lakers would trade at least two players to improve their playoff chances.

4.
purview n.

the range of operation, authority, control, concern, etc.

The police could not arrest him across the border since the next country was beyond their purview.

5.
pusillanimous adj.

lacking courage or resolution; cowardly; faint-hearted; timid

They cowered in front of the advancing troops and then ran away in a pusillanimous manner.

6.
pyre n.

a heap of combustibles arranged for burning a dead body

The Vikings had a tradition of placing a body on a floating funeral pyre, setting it aflame and putting it adrift into the ocean.

7.
quandary n.

a puzzling or difficult problem or situation

The men found themselves in a quandary, trapped in the jungle with few supplies and on the run from a hostile tribe.

8.
quixotic adj.

chivalrous or romantic to a ridiculous or extravagant degree

Henry had the quixotic notion that he could win the girl's attention if he could somehow rescue her from a blazing fire.

9.

raillery

n.

good-humored satire

My friends love to tease everyone around them, but I get annoyed by their constant raillery.

10.

rapacious

adj.

having the tendency to seize by violence or by unlawful or greedy methods

The rapacious pirates stole everything from the village, including all the pretty girls.

11.

redoubtable

adj.

formidable, causing fear; worthy of respect

The gladiator bowed as his redoubtable opponent, the seven-foot tall Persian general, entered the auditorium.

12.

refractory

adj.

resistant to authority or control

He had such a refractory case of the disease that we had to search the world to find a treatment that might offer some hope.

13.

remonstrate

v.

to plead in protest to those who have power to right or prevent a wrong

Rather than remonstrate through the legal system, the group decided to take their protest to the streets.

14.

reparation

n.

the act of making amends, as for an injury, loss, or wrong

It was decided by the Allied powers after the war that Germany would pay $33 billion in reparations for all the damage it had caused.

15.

repast

n.

a quantity of food taken or provided for one occasion of eating

After a very satisfying repast of turkey and wine, we settled down for an afternoon nap.

16.

repertoire

n.

the selection of songs, plays, or pieces known by a performer or group of performers

We were disappointed that the song "Brown Eyed Girl" was not in the musician's repertoire.

WEEK 1
WEEK 2
WEEK 3
WEEK 4
WEEK 5
WEEK 6
WEEK 7
WEEK 8
WEEK 9
WEEK 10

ADVANCED

17.

reprobate

n.

one abandoned to depravity and sin

Everyone shunned the reprobate since he was interested only in vices such as drinking and gambling.

18.

requiem

n.

a solemn song or poem written or performed for the dead

At the funeral, the quartet performed a requiem that brought everyone to tears.

19.

requite

v.

to repay either good or evil to

I was dismayed that the love poems I had written for Darlene were never requited with her affection.

20.

retinue

n.

the body of persons who attend a person of importance in travel or public appearance

The actor travels with a large retinue of bodyguards, hairdressers, wardrobe specialists, and close personal friends.

21.

rhapsodize

v.

to speak enthusiastically about; to give praise to

She wouldn't stop rhapsodizing about the apparently stunning performance she had seen at the Hollywood Bowl.

22.

ribald

adj.

indulging in or manifesting coarse indecency or obscenity

My parents were offended by the comedian's ribald sense of humor and use of foul language.

23.

ruffian

adj.

a lawless or recklessly brutal fellow

The ruffian kid always picked fights and stole money from those younger and smaller than himself.

24.

sagacious

adj.

having or showing acute mental discernment and keen practical sense; shrewd

The wizard was often sought for his sagacious advice by all the citizens of the lower village.

25.

salacious

adj.

stimulating sexual desire; lustful

I wasn't sure why she kept making such salacious comments, since she had told me several times she wasn't attracted to me.

26.

salient

adj.

standing out prominently

Even though the actor played only a supporting role in the film, his performance was the most salient one.

27.

salubrious

adj.

favorable to or promoting health; healthful

Barry's home provided, for him, the most salubrious atmosphere away from the rush and tumble world of investment banking.

28.

salutary

adj.

producing a beneficial result

Instead of holding a sour, negative air, you should look at the salutary benefits of staying after class.

29.

sapience

n.

deep wisdom or knowledge

The sermon was delivered with such sapience that I had to reconsider my previous assessment of the preacher as a buffoon.

30.

sardonic

adj.

scornfully or bitterly sarcastic

I found her sardonic wit amusing, but most people found her to be too bitter and critical.

31.

saturnine

adj.

sluggish in temperament; gloomy; taciturn

Known to have a saturnine disposition, Ted was not the most popular of people; he was simply never fun to be around, since he never seemed happy.

32.

savant

n.

a learned or scholarly person, especially one who is unexpectedly so

The high school dropout turned out to be quite a savant when it came to computer programming.

WEEK 1
WEEK 2
WEEK 3
WEEK 4
WEEK 5
WEEK 6
WEEK 7
WEEK 8
WEEK 9
WEEK 10

ADVANCED

33.
scintilla
n.

a minute particle; spark; trace

I haven't a scintilla of evidence that he committed the crime, but my gut feeling is that he was the perpetrator.

34.
sedulous
adj.

persistent in effort

The sedulous student never gave up trying to pass French, even after he failed it three times.

35.
senescent
adj.

growing old; aging

Hindered by ailing eyesight and diminishing mobility, my senescent father could no longer do many of the things he had once enjoyed.

36.
sibilant
adj.

made with a hissing sound

Whenever the girl wore her retainer, she spoke in a more sibilant and lisping way.

37.
solicitous
adj.

anxious or concerned; expressing care, sometimes in a too eager way

The solicitous nurse would not leave him alone, constantly checking on him to see if he was feeling okay.

38.
sonorous
adj.

producing full, deep, or rich sound

I just had my cello tuned, and now it is more sonorous than ever.

39.
splenetic
adj.

irritable; easily angered; spiteful

In an obviously splenetic moment, the press secretary snapped at the reporters for no apparent reason.

40.
staid
adj.

of settled or sedate character; not flighty or capricious

Whenever anything goes wrong, we look to Ivan because he remains calm and staid.

41.
stentorian   adj.

very loud or powerful in sound

The speaker's stentorian voice boomed over the loudspeakers, making all of us jump out of our skins.

42.
stipend   n.

a definite amount of compensation regularly paid, such as a salary or an allowance

While he was performing investigative work for the FBI, he was paid a stipend of five thousand dollars a week.

43.
stolid   adj.

having or expressing little emotion

Her father was a stolid man who never smiled and rarely spoke a kind word, even to those he loved.

44.
stultify   v.

to make ineffective; to cause to appear foolish

My debate opponent was effective at stultifying me whenever I tried to make my arguments.

45.
subterranean   adj.

existing, situated, or operating below the surface of the earth; underground

Moles and groundhogs are subterranean creatures, coming out of their underground dens to forage for food.

46.
suffuse   v.

to spread through or over, as with liquid, color, or light

The room was suffused with the pale light of the rising sun.

47.
supine   adj.

lying on the back; expressing indifference or inactivity

Struck a fatal blow by Achilles' sword, he fell supine, his eyes glassy and staring upward into the night's sky.

48.
surrogate   n.

one that is substituted for or appointed to act in place of another

The surrogate mother was paid a hefty sum for the temporary use of her womb.

WEEK 1
WEEK 2
WEEK 3
WEEK 4
WEEK 5
WEEK 6
WEEK 7
WEEK 8
WEEK 9
WEEK 10

ADVANCED

49.

table   v.

to postpone consideration of,
especially of legislation

I think it would be best if we just table the issue until there is a more convenient time for us to discuss it.

50.

tantamount   adj.

equivalent, as in value, force, effect,
or significance

Spying for the enemy and selling state secrets is tantamount to contributing to the deaths of hundreds of your countrymen.

A. Fill in the appropriate words using the clues below.

across:

2) n. the act of making amends, as for an injury, loss, or wrong
4) adj. resistant to authority or control
6) adj. of settled or sedate character; not flighty or capricious
8) adj. lacking courage or resolution; cowardly; faint-hearted; timid
9) v. to steal, often in violation of trust
10) adj. persistent in effort

down:

1) adj. stimulating sexual desire; lustful
3) adj. scornfully or bitterly sarcastic
5) adj. favorable to or promoting health; healthful
7) adj. lying on the back; expressing indifference or inactivity

B. Match the words on the left with their appropriate definitions on the right.

A. punctilious _____ 1. adj. indulging in or manifesting coarse indecency or obscenity

B. purported _____ 2. adj. producing full, deep, or rich sound

C. quandary _____ 3. n. the body of persons who attend a person of importance in travel or public appearance

D. quixotic _____ 4. v. to spread through or over, as with liquid, color, or light

E. rapacious _____ 5. v. to plead in protest to those who have power to right or prevent a wrong

F. remonstrate _____ 6. adj. standing out prominently

G. repast _____ 7. adj. having or expressing little emotion

H. reprobate _____ 8. adj. chivalrous or romantic to a ridiculous or extravagant degree

I. requiem _____ 9. adj. extremely attentive to details, esp. those related to formalities or proper conduct

J. retinue _____ 10. n. one abandoned to depravity and sin

K. ribald _____ 11. adj. having the tendency to seize by violence or by unlawful or greedy methods

L. sagacious _____ 12. adj. anxious or concerned; expressing care, sometimes in a too eager way

M. salient _____ 13. adj. reputed or claimed; alleged

N. saturnine _____ 14. n. a solemn song or poem written or performed for the dead

O. savant _____ 15. n. a puzzling or difficult problem or situation

P. sibilant _____ 16. adj. made with a hissing sound

Q. solicitous _____ 17. n. a learned or scholarly person, especially one who is unexpectedly so

R. sonorous _____ 18. adj. sluggish in temperament; gloomy; taciturn

S. stolid _____ 19. adj. having or showing acute mental discernment and keen practical sense; shrewd

T. suffuse _____ 20. n. a quantity of food taken or provided for one occasion of eating

WEEK 1
WEEK 2
WEEK 3
WEEK 4
WEEK 5
WEEK 6
WEEK 7
WEEK 8
WEEK 9
WEEK 10
ADVANCED

300pts

100pts

Week 10

wean

virile

verb

adj.

"Do a little more each day than you think you possibly can."
- Lowell Thomas

Start   Restart

1.
taut
adj.

stretched tight

The fishing line went taut when he hooked a huge trout.

2.
tautology
n.

a redundancy

The teacher pointed out several tautologies in the student's essay, in which the student merely repeated what he had just said!

3.
tempestuous
adj.

characterized by or subject to a violent commotion or disturbance

The wind was tempestuous as it blew strongly down the canyon, knocking down many trees that evening.

4.
temporize
v.

to pursue a policy of delay

The generals valiantly temporized in order to delay the enemy while their men devised a plan for invasion.

5.
tendentious
adj.

marked by a strongly implicit partisan point of view

The old woman made tendentious but unsupported assertions regarding the authenticity of her painting, which she claimed to be a Van Gogh.

6.
tenor
n.

the general sense of or course of thought running through something written or spoken

The tenor of the conversation was not heading in the direction I had hoped for, so I tried my best to change the topic.

7.
threadbare
adj.

meager, poor, scanty

The beggar's threadbare clothing made it evident that he had no money and no home.

8.
timbre
n.

the quality of a tone, as distinguished by intensity and pitch

The timbre of Renee Fleming's heavenly voice is unmistakable, so she is rightfully one of the most famous sopranos in the world today.

WEEK 1
WEEK 2
WEEK 3
WEEK 4
WEEK 5
WEEK 6
WEEK 7
WEEK 8
WEEK 9
WEEK 10

ADVANCED

9.
titillate
v.

to stimulate by touching lightly; to tickle

These diamond earrings were designed to titillate the fancy of women with the means to buy them.

10.
titular
adj.

bearing a title; having power in name only

Several European nations still allow a kings or queens to rule as titular sovereigns, even though they hold no actual decision-making powers.

11.
tonic
n.

a refreshing or restorative beverage

Snake oil was once a popular tonic thought to cure a host of common maladies, from baldness to depression.

12.
traipse
v.

to walk or go aimlessly or idly or without finding or reaching one's goal; (n.) a tiring walk

Jill and Gillian traipsed through the woods like a couple of young fawns.

13.
trammel
n.

a restraint; something that restricts movement or progress

Some tribes never advance into the 21st century because they are bound by the trammels of custom.

14.
transverse
adj.

lying or being across in a crosswise direction

We ordered the beams of the new house to be situated transverse to the old ones, but the carpenters laid them out in a parallel fashion instead.

15.
treatise
n.

an elaborate literary composition presenting a subject in all its parts

The scholar spent a lifetime writing a comprehensive treatise on the importance of democracy in America.

16.
trove
n.

a collection of objects, especially a valuable one

We were surprised to find that the old shack contained a trove of wealth from various parts of the world.

17.

turpitude

n.

corruption; wickedness

Senator McCarthy denounced the moral turpitude of all the suspected Communists in the hearing.

18.

umbrage

n.

offense, resentment

The famous writer took great umbrage at the scathing reviews of his new book.

19.

unction

n.

the act of anointing with oil as part of a religious ceremony

The ceremony of unction is a rite given by a priest to those dying, using oil to bless the person before they pass away.

20.

unctuous

adj.

oily; exaggerated and false sincerity

The unctuous banker was excessively flattering to those more powerful than he, but everybody thought him highly insincere.

21.

unflagging

adj.

not stopping; untiring

If we want to succeed in life, we must face all our difficulties with unflagging determination.

22.

ungainly

adj.

not graceful; awkward; unwieldy; clumsy; (adv.) in an awkward manner

The giant walked into the city in a slow, ungainly manner, weaving side to side as he crushed each small cottage.

23.

unwieldy

adj.

moved or managed with difficulty, as from great size or awkward shape

Since we could not find our unwieldy parcel in the baggage claim carousel, it had to be claimed at the oversized luggage counter.

24.

unwonted

adj.

not habitual; unusual

The unwonted tenderness from my mother was quite a departure from her usual harshness.

WEEK 1
WEEK 2
WEEK 3
WEEK 4
WEEK 5
WEEK 6
WEEK 7
WEEK 8
WEEK 9
WEEK 10
ADVANCED

25.
upbraid
v.

to criticize sharply

The boss upbraided his interns and subordinates whenever he had a bad day.

26.
usurp
v.

to take possession of by force

The devious prince usurped the throne by force, exiled the royal family to Siberia, and reigned as an unlawful king for twenty years.

27.
usury
n.

loaning money at a rate of interest beyond what is allowed by law

My father wanted to report the loan shark for usury, but he needed the money desperately and simply had to pay the ridiculously high interest.

28.
utilitarian
adj.

having regard for something's usefulness rather than its beauty or ornamentation; (n.) an advocate of the belief that the value of something is determined by its utility

He built the house rather plainly, more concerned about its utilitarian purposes than any aesthetic pleasure it might bring.

29.
vacuous
adj.

empty and meaningless

His sisters' vacuous discussions about table linens and laundry soaps bored Tom.

30.
vagary
n.

an extravagant or erratic idea or action

One could only explain the purchase of the huge farm as one of her vagaries, which inexplicably possessed her every once in a while.

31.
vassal
n.

a slave or bondman

Lord Bunsbury was generous to his vassals, deeding each family living on his estate several acres of rich, tillable land.

32.
venal
adj.

corrupt, willing to accept bribes

The venal police officer took money from those wealthy enough to pay him to avoid being arrested.

33.

veracious adj.

habitually disposed to speak the truth

The veracious little girl never told a lie, often noting early stories of George Washington's honesty.

34.

verdant adj.

green with vegetation

The bare, dusty stretch of desert was transformed by spring rain into a verdant field of wildflowers.

35.

vernacular n.

the language of one's country or region; the everyday language of a people; common expressions

The vernacular of the deep South is so peculiar that other people may have difficulty understanding it.

36.

vernal adj.

belonging to or suggestive of the spring

Vivaldi's "Four Seasons," especially "Spring" is a distinctively beautiful and decidedly vernal composition, as suggested by the title.

37.

vestment n.

clothing or covering, especially a robe that denotes a rank or position

The priest accidentally spilled an entire chalice of sacramental wine on his brand new vestments.

38.

vicissitude n.

one of the sudden or unexpected changes that occur in one's life

The vicissitudes of misfortune over the years resulted in the loss of the family's wealth.

39.

vignette n.

a short scene or incident, as one within a movie; an oval picture having a background that is shaded off gradually

The art school student drew exquisite vignettes to be used as table centerpieces at the event.

40.

virile adj.

masculine

Many men at Muscle Beach look quite virile with their bulging biceps and rippled abs.

WEEK 1
WEEK 2
WEEK 3
WEEK 4
WEEK 5
WEEK 6
WEEK 7
WEEK 8
WEEK 9
WEEK 10
ADVANCED

41.
viscous
adj.

thick and sticky

The viscous honey flowed very slowly out of the jar and into my cup.

42.
vitiate
v.

to reduce the quality of a substance; to corrupt; to invalidate

The unfortunate scandal vitiated the young celebrity's confidence, making it impossible for him to resurrect his career.

43.
vituperative
adj.

using harshly abusive criticism

The young gang member's vituperative words earned him a lecture from the judge and a long sentence in jail.

44.
vivify
v.

to imbue with life; to make lively

We tried to vivify the sad, grieving widow by buying her a vacation to St. Tropez for the summer.

45.
vociferate
v.

to protest loudly and vehemently

An individual may need to vociferate his or her concerns to make sure they are heard and addressed.

46.
vogue
n.

the prevalent way or fashion

Some people feel the need to read fashion magazines to find out what is in vogue.

47.
voluble
adj.

having great fluency in speaking

As a voluble man, the Speaker of the House habitually made speeches so natural and eloquent that he moved some to tears.

48.
wanton
adj.

immoral or unchaste; rude

Billy fell under the spell of the wanton temptress and lost all of his earnings in one night.

WEEK
1

WEEK
2

WEEK
3

WEEK
4

WEEK
5

WEEK
6

WEEK
7

WEEK
8

WEEK
9

WEEK
10

49.

wean v.

to transfer (the young) from dependence on mother's milk to another form of nourishment

The mother cat weaned her kittens by pushing them away from her when they attempted to nurse.

50.

zephyr n.

any soft, gentle wind, especially one from the west

The zephyr blew in, gently rocking the cradle on the porch and stirring the tree branches in our yard.

A. Fill in the appropriate words using the clues below.

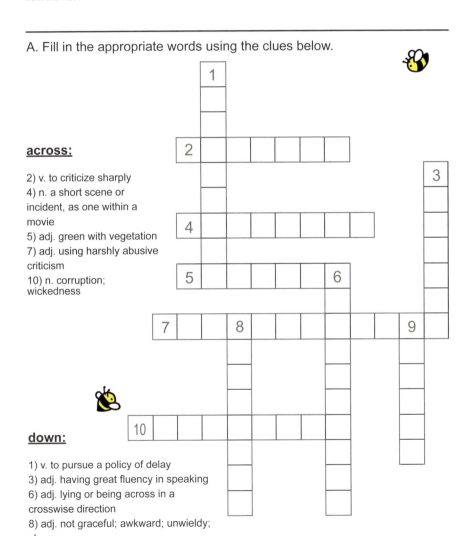

across:

2) v. to criticize sharply
4) n. a short scene or incident, as one within a movie
5) adj. green with vegetation
7) adj. using harshly abusive criticism
10) n. corruption; wickedness

down:

1) v. to pursue a policy of delay
3) adj. having great fluency in speaking
6) adj. lying or being across in a crosswise direction
8) adj. not graceful; awkward; unwieldy; clumsy
9) n. an extravagant or erratic idea or action

B. Match the words on the left with their appropriate definitions on the right.

A. tempestuous _____ 1. adj. not habitual; unusual

B. titillate _____ 2. n. offense, resentment

C. traipse _____ 3. n. an elaborate literary composition presenting a subject in all its parts

D. treatise _____ 4. adj. characterized by or subject to a violent commotion or disturbance

E. umbrage _____ 5. adj. moved or managed with difficulty, as from great size or awkward shape

F. unctuous _____ 6. adj. not stopping; untiring

G. unflagging _____ 7. n. one of the sudden or unexpected changes that occur in one's life

H. unwieldy _____ 8. adj. habitually disposed to speak the truth

I. unwonted _____ 9. adj. oily; exaggerated and false sincerity

J. usurp _____ 10. v. to protest loudly and vehemently

K. utilitarian _____ 11. adj. immoral or unchaste; rude

L. vacuous _____ 12. adj. empty and meaningless

M. venal _____ 13. n. the language of one's country or region; the everyday language of a people; common expressions

N. veracious _____ 14. adj. thick and sticky

O. vernacular _____ 15. v. to stimulate by touching lightly; to tickle

P. vicissitude _____ 16. adj. having regard for its usefulness rather than its beauty or ornamentation

Q. virile _____ 17. adj. corrupt, willing to accept bribes

R. viscous _____ 18. adj. masculine

S. vociferate _____ 19. v. to take possession of by force

T. wanton _____ 20. v. to walk or go aimlessly or idly or without finding or reaching one's goal; n. a tiring walk

Answer Keys

Regular Level

Week 1	Week 2	Week 3	Week 4	Week 5
1. R	1. I	1. S	1. C	1. N
2. P	2. O	2. E	2. H	2. P
3. K	3. C	3. K	3. P	3. D
4. S	4. S	4. N	4. A	4. G
5. E	5. B	5. C	5. L	5. C
6. Q	6. K	6. G	6. T	6. O
7. A	7. M	7. J	7. B	7. M
8. O	8. A	8. Q	8. G	8. L
9. T	9. N	9. H	9. I	9. Q
10. D	10. D	10. F	10. E	10. F
11. F	11. G	11. I	11. F	11. I
12. H	12. F	12. P	12. M	12. A
13. J	13. T	13. B	13. Q	13. K
14. I	14. E	14. L	14. S	14. E
15. B	15. L	15. O	15. R	15. B
16. N	16. P	16. M	16. O	16. J
17. L	17. R	17. D	17. N	17. R
18. G	18. H	18. T	18. K	18. T
19. M	19. J	19. A	19. D	19. H
20. C	20. Q	20. R	20. J	20. S

Week 6	Week 7	Week 8	Week 9	Week 10
1. K	1. E	1. M	1. T	1. T
2. J	2. O	2. C	2. S	2. E
3. E	3. C	3. I	3. Q	3. C
4. M	4. N	4. N	4. D	4. P
5. D	5. K	5. J	5. B	5. J
6. O	6. A	6. O	6. K	6. H
7. I	7. B	7. S	7. C	7. I
8. F	8. M	8. A	8. J	8. K
9. R	9. T	9. R	9. N	9. Q
10. Q	10. Q	10. B	10. P	10. B
11. A	11. D	11. D	11. A	11. M
12. G	12. F	12. K	12. I	12. R
13. B	13. L	13. G	13. O	13. S
14. H	14. R	14. T	14. G	14. O
15. N	15. H	15. E	15. H	15. N
16. L	16. S	16. F	16. L	16. L
17. T	17. J	17. Q	17. E	17. G
18. P	18. I	18. L	18. M	18. A
19. S	19. G	19. H	19. R	19. F
20. C	20. P	20. P	20. F	20. D

Regular Level
Crossword Puzzle

Week 1

```
                    A
                    C
          A         E     A
          S   S     R     D
          S   S     B     R
          S   I     I     O
      A   B   D   I   C   A   T   E
      N   U           L   I
  A   U   D   A   C   I   O   U   S
      T   O           T   O
      I   S       A   R   D   E   N   T
      T           C
      H       B   A   N   T   E   R
  B   E   L   L   I   C   O   S   E
      I           T
      S           I
                  O
                  N
```

Week 2

```
                          B
                          E
                          N
          C   H   R   O   N   I   C       C
                  O           G           O
      C   A   C   O   P   H   O   N   Y   N
      O           P       C   O   H   E   S   I   V   E
      M           L       O           M
      P           C   O   N   N   I   V   E
      L           I       V           O
      I           O       E           R
      C           U       R       C   H   A   S   T   E
      I           S       G           N
      T                   E           E
      Y                               O
                                      U
                                      S
```

Week 3

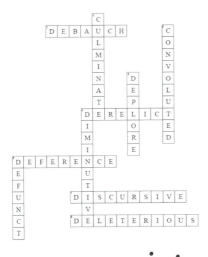

```
                  C
      D   E   B   A   U   C   H           C
                  L                       O
                  M                       N
                  I           D           V
                  N           E           O
                  A           P           L
                  T       D   E   R   E   L   I   C   T
              D   I           O           T
              I   M           R           E
              M   I           E           D
      D   E   F   E   R   E   N   C   E
      E           U
      F           T
      U       D   I   S   C   U   R   S   I   V   E
      N           V
      C       D   E   L   E   T   E   R   I   O   U   S
      T
```

Week 4

```
          E   B   U   L   L   I   E   N   T
                          X               D
                          P               I
          E   L   U   C   I   D   A   T   E   S   T
          D               D               R
          I               I               R
          F               E               A
          Y       E   X   T   R   A   N   E   O   U   S
                  N           C           G
      D   I   V   E   S   T   Y           H
                  U                       T
              E   X   I   G   E   N   T
                  M
                  I
                  T
```

245

Regular Level Crossword Puzzle

Week 5

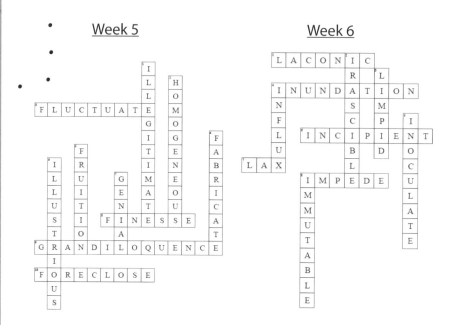

Week 6

Week 7

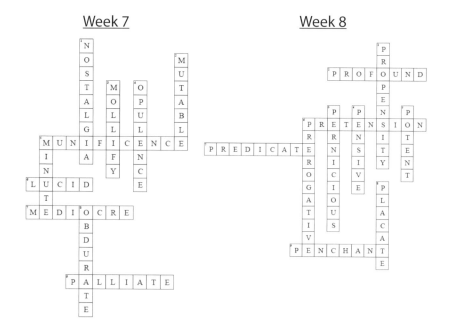

Week 8

Regular Level
Crossword Puzzle

Week 9

Week 10

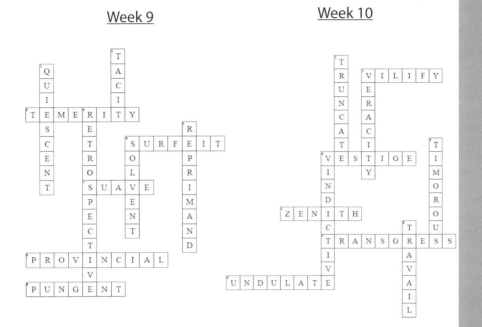

Advanced Level

Week 1	Week 2	Week 3	Week 4	Week 5
1. S	1. M	1. A	1. O	1. G
2. Q	2. R	2. E	2. R	2. P
3. I	3. I	3. L	3. N	3. S
4. K	4. F	4. R	4. G	4. B
5. J	5. H	5. F	5. E	5. M
6. L	6. E	6. G	6. T	6. R
7. O	7. L	7. S	7. F	7. N
8. H	8. P	8. D	8. M	8. K
9. B	9. K	9. P	9. D	9. F
10. E	10. T	10. J	10. C	10. D
11. N	11. A	11. I	11. B	11. L
12. T	12. Q	12. T	12. H	12. C
13. D	13. J	13. H	13. K	13. E
14. M	14. O	14. M	14. L	14. J
15. R	15. C	15. K	15. I	15. I
16. A	16. N	16. N	16. J	16. T
17. G	17. S	17. Q	17. P	17. H
18. F	18. D	18. C	18. Q	18. O
19. C	19. B	19. B	19. S	19. A
20. P	20. G	20. O	20. A	20. Q

Week 6	Week 7	Week 8	Week 9	Week 10
1. A	1. A	1. B	1. K	1. I
2. B	2. M	2. N	2. R	2. E
3. F	3. T	3. C	3. J	3. D
4. I	4. O	4. J	4. T	4. A
5. G	5. P	5. T	5. F	5. H
6. S	6. F	6. Q	6. M	6. G
7. E	7. I	7. S	7. S	7. P
8. L	8. R	8. L	8. D	8. N
9. T	9. E	9. A	9. A	9. F
10. D	10. D	10. O	10. H	10. S
11. O	11. C	11. I	11. E	11. T
12. R	12. K	12. D	12. Q	12. L
13. C	13. H	13. K	13. B	13. O
14. N	14. J	14. E	14. I	14. R
15. P	15. N	15. F	15. C	15. B
16. Q	16. S	16. M	16. P	16. K
17. J	17. Q	17. H	17. O	17. M
18. K	18. L	18. R	18. N	18. Q
19. M	19. B	19. P	19. L	19. J
20. H	20. G	20. G	20. G	20. C

Advanced Level
Crossword Puzzle

Week 1

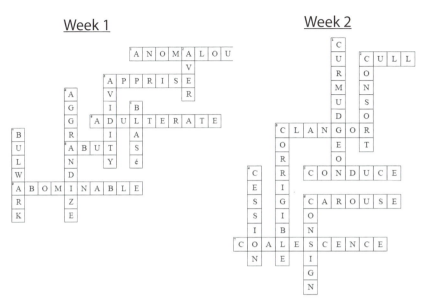

```
              A N O M A L O U S
                      V
          A P P R I S E R
       A              V
       G              E
       G      A D U L T E R A T E
       R      B
 B     A  B U T  S
 U     N       A  S
 L     D       Y  é
 W
 A B O M I N A B L E
 R     Z
 K     E
```

Week 2

```
              C
              U        C U L L
              R        O
              M        N
              U        S
              D        O
         C L A N G O R T
         O    R        T
         R    E
 C       R    O
 E       I  C O N D U C E
 S       G
 S       I  C A R O U S E
 I       B  O
 C O A L E S C E N C E
 N       E  I
              G
              N
```

Week 3

```
            D
 D I S S E N T I O U S
            N
 D I C T U M
            D
 E        E S C A P A D E
 F        I
 E F F I C A C I O U S
 R        A        D
 O      E F F E T E E
 N        F        M
 T        E
 E        C
 R    D E N O T E
 Y
```

Week 4

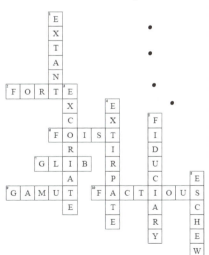

```
 E
 X
 T
 A
 N
 F O R T E
 X        E
 C        X      F
 F O I S T I      I
 R        R      D
 G L I B  P      U
 A        R      C    E
 G A M U T E  F A C T I O U S
 E        F A    A    C
              T      R    H
              E      Y    E
                          W
```

Advanced Level Crossword Puzzle

Week 5

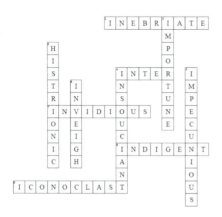

Week 6

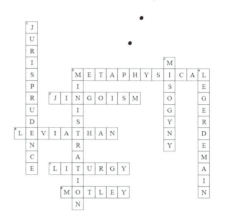

Week 7

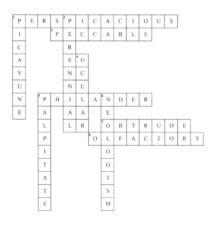

Week 8

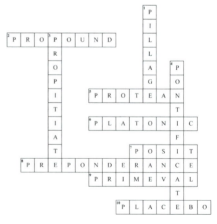

Advanced Level
Crossword Puzzle

Week 9

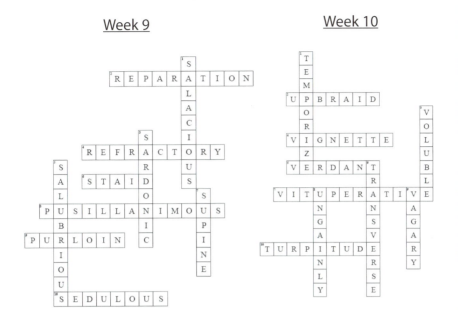

Week 10